RAMSB[

A Wiltshire village and its airfield

At War

1939-1945

ROGER DAY

Published by ROGER DAY,
77 Chilton Way,
Hungerford, Berkshire RG17 0JF.

First published 1999.

ISBN 0 9536601 0 9

Printed in England.

Design and Cartography; Roger and Christopher Day.

Designed and produced by
Axxent Ltd
The Short Run Book Company
St Stephen's House
Arthur Road,
Windsor, Berkshire SL4 1RY

(Front cover) *Ramsbury airfield, early June 1944. (Imperial War Museum)*
(Previous page) *Brookside Cottage, Newtown Road, on a glorious summers day in 1944. Miss Woolford, who lived in the cottage at that time, proudly shows an interested American air force officer her beautiful garden. (Mrs V. Barnard via Mrs R. Connor)*

Table of contents

Preface and acknowledgements   **5**

Introduction   **7**

Chapter one – The village gears up for war   **11**
Air raid precautions   13
The Police   16
The Fire Service   18
Ramsbury Home Guard   20
Aldbourne Home Guard   25
Chilton Foliat Home Guard   28
Chilton Aircraft Home Guard   29
The Air Training Corps   30

Chapter two – Lend a hand on the land   **35**
Farming   37
Prisoners of war   39

Chapter three – Friendly invaders   **49**
Worcester Terriers   51
The Americans   54
The Paras   70

Chapter four – Ramsbury airfield   **73**
Construction phase   75
Eighth USAAF arrive   81
RAF pilot training   83
437th TCG move in   93
The final years   115

Chapter five – Ramsbury today   **119**
Victory at last   121

Appendix one   **125**

Appendix two   **129**

Bibliography   **133**

Preface and Acknowledgements

This book owes its origin to the many questions about wartime Ramsbury that I asked my parents as a young child. As far as I can recall the replies I received never fully satisfied my curiosity, and as the years passed by so my determination to set on record this period of local history grew.

I have been very fortunate over the years to have made contact with a number of veterans, both civilian and military, who still have vivid memories of this area during World War Two. I should like to express here my sincere appreciation to all who responded patiently to my questions and who took the time and trouble to send me written accounts, original documentary material and of course photographs, without which this book would be far less complete.

In all books of this type, that rely on personal recollections, errors and discrepancies are bound to occur. Wherever possible I have tried to ensure the accuracy of these accounts and therefore accept full responsibility for any errors that may be present.

Official information used in this book has been extracted from records held by the Public Record Office at Kew, the RAF Museum at Hendon, the Wiltshire County Record Office at Trowbridge and the USAAF Historic Record Center at Maxwell AFB. All Crown Copyright material is reproduced with the permission of the controller of Her Majesty's Stationery Office.

Individual thanks are extended to the following: John Aitken, Oliver Atkins, Tom Averill, Fred Bahlau, Peter 'Jake' Baldwin, Doug Barnes, David Bartter, Ernest 'Bill' Berry, Mike Berry, Joe Beyrle, Donald Bolce, Joe Bowes, Albert Brothers, Jim Carter, Roger Coleson, Rosemary Connor, Ivan Cooke, Flo Cound, John Day, Max Demuth, Moya Dixon, Margaret Donovan, Leo Dopson, Bob Dunning, George 'Doc' Dwyer, Alice Edwards, Ted Farley, Doris Fielding, Henry Fimmer, Irmgard Graham, Frank Guild, Malcolm Harding-Roberts, Saul Harris, Geoffrey Haworth, Brian Holtam, 'Paddy' Hopkins, Gerald Jerram, Mr L.B. Jones, David Kady, George Lang, Ron Liddiard, Daphne Ludlow, Peter Ludlow, Percy Luker, Molly Lunn, Don March, Francesc Mazzotta, Ivan Mehoskey, Jack Merrick, Peter Mills, Gilbert Morton, Arthur Palmer, Cyril Palmer, Ted Pilgram, John Plenderleith, Rene Plenderleith, Tom Parsons, Robert Rader, John Reeder, Grp. Cpt. George Reid, George Rosie, Ron Scott, Ed Shames, Jim Skidmore, Gordon Starling, John Starling, Ken Trego, Charles Waltman, 'Tiny' Watts, Robert Webb, Guy Wentworth, Ron Westall, Jack Whipple, Joe Wilkins, 'Harry' Williams and Stephen Williams.

Thanks are also due to the many people who contributed cherished photographs from their family albums, and who are individually acknowledged adjacent to each caption.

Particular mention must be made of the assistance given by Barbara Croucher, Don Summers, and John Wadsworth who have each read the manuscript several times and made many important changes. My son Christopher also spent many hours drawing maps, developing black and white photographs, and trying to interpret and type my often illegible and miss-spelt script.

Finally very special thanks are extended to Neil Stevens of the Wilts and Berks ETO Research Group. I have had the privilege of knowing Neil for a decade or more. His particular area of interest lies with the numerous American units which were based in Wiltshire and Berkshire during World War Two. He has provided many photographs from his extensive collection, and other additional material for chapters three and four. His enthusiasm for the subject and interest in my book has been an inspiration. Neil, once again, thanks!

To conclude, I ask any readers who may have additional contributions, great or small, to write to me so that the information may be included in any further editions of this book.

Roger Day

Hungerford, Berkshire.   July 1999.

Introduction

The ancient village of Ramsbury nestles in the north east corner of Wiltshire beside the clear waters of the River Kennet. For centuries cattle have grazed the lush green water meadows, sheep have wandered on the high downs surrounding the village, and in the fields between man has tilled the soil. Until as recently as 1986 the main focal point was an old elm tree, which had reputedly stood in the Square for nearly three hundred years. There is however evidence that a community had existed here for more than a thousand years before the tree took root. Throughout history the village has sent its share of young sons to fight the nation's wars in far-off places; the memorial in the High Street records that 65 local men lost their lives in the 1914-1918 conflict. But this was a quiet, pastoral place, where for the most part, lives were ordered and little excitement ever intruded.

The Industrial Revolution passed Ramsbury by and neither the canal nor railway scarred the village or its surroundings. Even twenty years after the First World War horse drawn vehicles were still an essential part of every day life. The population, over 2,000 at one time, had by the late 1930s dropped to around 1,500. Everybody seemed to know each other's business in this well established, close-knit Wiltshire village.

On Sunday, 3rd September 1939, this rural idyll was rudely shattered when people in towns and villages all over the country heard the news which would change the course of their lives. On that day those near a radio heard the Prime Minister, Neville Chamberlain, solemnly announce that Britain was at war with Germany.

It was the start of six years of blackouts, rationing, air-raid warnings, of loved ones being sent away, and of the intensifying of community spirit which always seems to develop in times of trouble. The arrival of the Americans was for some the only bright spot in an otherwise miserable war.

On the following pages I have tried to record some of the events that occurred in this tiny corner of Britain during that traumatic period; the Home Guard, the Civil Defence, the construction and use of the airfield and the friendly 'military invasions'. Although the book looks primarily at the village, it also includes details of other war-time activity in the surrounding area, which I feel helps complete the story, since all were to play a significant part in Ramsbury's war.

A tranquil scene taken in Ramsbury during the 1920s. (Via J. Day)

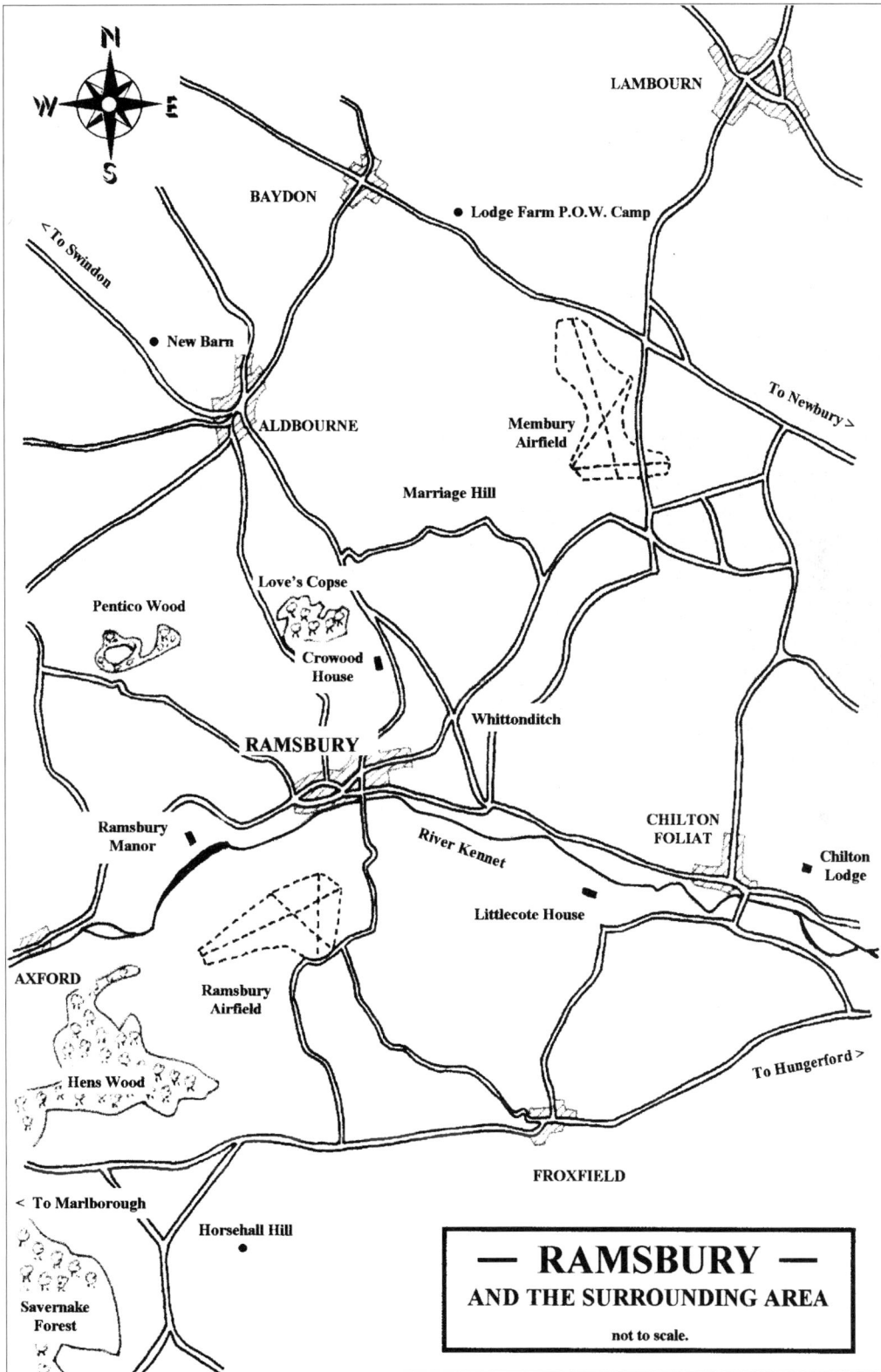

N W E S

LAMBOURN

BAYDON

● Lodge Farm P.O.W. Camp

< To Swindon

● New Barn

To Newbury >

ALDBOURNE

Membury Airfield

Marriage Hill

Love's Copse

Pentico Wood

Crowood House

Whittonditch

RAMSBURY

Ramsbury Manor

River Kennet

CHILTON FOLIAT

Chilton Lodge

Littlecote House

AXFORD

Ramsbury Airfield

To Hungerford >

Hens Wood

FROXFIELD

< To Marlborough

Horsehall Hill

Savernake Forest

— RAMSBURY —
AND THE SURROUNDING AREA
not to scale.

CHAPTER 1

THE VILLAGE GEARS UP FOR WAR

Air Raid Precautions

The ARP Act of 1937 called for the establishment of an Air Raid Precautions (ARP) Service controlled by the local authorities. During the following two years the service was brought into being and began preparing for the worst. In Ramsbury the members, all volunteers, performed their duties during evenings and at weekends, and at first it was difficult persuading a disinterested population to take ARP instructions seriously.

On Saturday, 8th July 1939 the first blackout exercise was organised in the village. The ARP teams under Chief Warden Mr J.H. Lawrence were all at their posts, as were the Special Police under Sergeant Painter. By midnight not a single light could be seen, and it was quiet enough for one warden to hear the air-raid siren in Marlborough.

The use of mustard gas in the First World War gave rise, during the 1930s, to fears that this weapon would be used against the civilian population in a future conflict. By the summer of 1939 the whole country had realised that war with Germany was imminent, and with that came a greater interest in individual protection against gas attacks. On the evening of Friday, 25th August 1939 at the Memorial Hall, local wardens had been very busy assembling and issuing gas masks (officially known as respirators), and the villagers were instructed to carry them at all times – although it was thought that fewer than one in five actually did so.

The ARP service had numerous duties and responsibilities, but without doubt the most important was to provide warning to the civilian population of air-raids. In large towns this warning was given by a wailing siren, however in rural communities a warden would cycle around blowing short blasts on a whistle. If poisonous gas was suspected the warning would be given by means of hand rattles, and once the danger had passed the 'All Clear' was signalled by ringing a hand bell. The wardens soon discovered that their task would be greatly simplified if they formed a closer working relationship with the police – easily arranged since the Wiltshire ARP Controller was also the county's Chief Constable.

Another large scale exercise took place on the evening of Wednesday, 8th May 1940. In addition to the wardens, the Boy Scouts were involved (acting as casualties), and also the Auxiliary Fire Service and the Special Police. The simulated events included an incendiary bomb at the west end of the village and a high explosive bomb in Blind Lane. The major lesson learnt from this exercise was that more stretchers were needed!

Fortunately the village was never deliberately bombed. However during the Blitz, which embraced the winter of 1940–1941, the Luftwaffe frequently 'visited' places such as Bath, Bristol and Coventry, and Ramsbury's wardens would always be held at a high state of alert, as many of the German raiders would fly over the village on their way to or from these targets. During this period a bomb fell at the bottom of White Hill, near Axford, but fortunately failed to explode. To deal with any incendiaries which may have fallen on to the parish church, wire netting was placed over the roof and tower in an attempt to prevent bombs from lodging there. In addition a series of ladders were erected to help ARP teams reach the roof quickly and extinguish any fire.

Once the blackout regulations came into force it was an offence to show a light after dark, and this rule was strictly enforced. Many local drapery stores, such as Mr Harrison's establishment in the High Street, did a roaring trade selling heavy dark material which householders made into 'black-out' curtains. Most people found the regulations very

Ramsbury had two ARP sections. This group was photographed at the school during 1944. (Miss A. Edwards)
H. Edwards   C. Jenawy   L. Kimber   W. Wootton   F. Chamberlain   G. Alder
G. Chamberlain   L. Lawrence   W. Calvert   ?. Giddings

In charge of the above section was Mr W.A. Smith who ran a gent's hairdressing business from his home in the High Street, where this photograph was taken. (Mrs R. Connor)
F. Smith   C. Giddings   ?. Brown   H. Woolford   T. Woolford   A. Franklin   A. Barnes   J. Penny
?. Harris   T. Ray   A. Childs   W.A. Smith   E. Lawrence   J. Franklin   ?. Hobbs

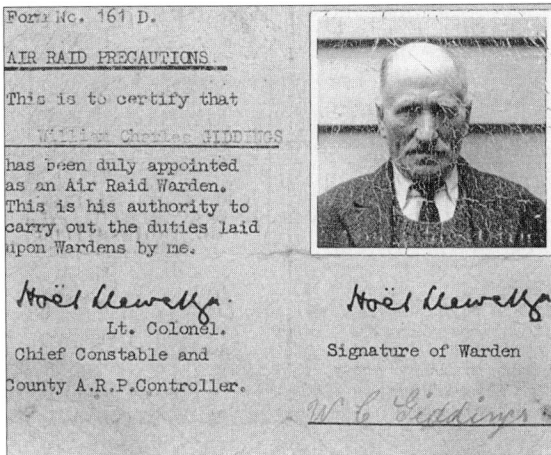

Form No. 161 D.

AIR RAID PRECAUTIONS.

This is to certify that

~~William Chester GIDDINGS~~

has been duly appointed as an Air Raid Warden. This is his authority to carry out the duties laid upon Wardens by me.

Noël Llewellyn

Lt. Colonel.
Chief Constable and County A.R.P.Controller.

Noël Llewellyn

Signature of Warden

W C Giddings

(Above) An Air Raid Warden's warrant card issued on 17th October 1940 to Mr W.C. Giddings of Whittonditch Road. *(via Mrs R. Plenderleith)*

(Right) Mr W.A. Smith pictured in his anti-gas suit (light). It was designed for men employed in gas decontamination squads. Made of oil skin it was normally worn in conjunction with rubber boots, gas mask, and a hood. Mr Smith became Chief Warden in Ramsbury after the unfortunate death, at an early age, of Mr J.H. Lawrence. (Mrs R. Connor)

This group of people represented most of Ramsbury's Civil Defence organisation. The photograph was taken in the school playground. Note the Civil Defence armbands worn by the two ladies on the extreme right. (via Mrs R. Connor)

inconvenient, and to help them find their way in the dark white paint was liberally applied to virtually every solid object. Kerbs and steps were edged with paint and trees, lamp posts and telegraph poles were decorated with white bands.

In August 1941 a new civilian organisation was created, which was to be known as the Fire Guard. This force was directed and co-ordinated by the ARP wardens and its duties were to watch the fall of fire bombs, to warn the local population if appropriate, and to prevent small fires from spreading. Those not already involved in Civil Defence duties were required to take their turn as Fire Guards, and although the organisation eventually became the largest of the Civil Defence services, the duty was always unpopular.

In September 1941, the ARP and fire services were reorganised into a single structure called 'Civil Defence'. The village came within the boundaries of No. 7 South Western Civil Defence Region, with regional headquarters in Bristol.

Ramsbury also provided members for the British Red Cross, the Woman's Institute and The Woman's Voluntary Service. In 1940 women of the village set up a 'Spitfire for Wiltshire' fund and by 20th January 1941, as a result of calling on every house in the Parish, an amount of £138-5s-4½d was raised. This was forwarded directly to Lord Beaverbrook, the Minister for Aircraft Production.

In April 1945, with the war in Europe almost at an end, the Civil Defence services had to stand-down, finally being disbanded in June of that year.

The Police

With the outbreak of war enormous extra responsibilities were thrust upon the Police Force. To help with the workload the Auxiliary Police War Reserve was called upon. The War Reserve, which had been recruited before hostilities began, was a full-time force consisting mainly of retired policemen who were expected to work alongside their colleagues from the regular constabulary. In addition duties were shared by part-time Special Police Constables, large numbers of whom were employed, as may be seen from the caption.

Ramsbury's resident police officer at the outbreak of war was Sgt. Painter who was based in Oxford Street. A radio broadcast by Anthony Eden on Tuesday, 14th May 1940, called for men to join the Local Defence Volunteers and requested that all those interested should report to their local police station. As a result Sgt. Painter was inundated with volunteers the following day and men were still applying to join a week later.

The large number of officers recruited in relation to the village's size (population 1,575 in 1939) was surprising and, complaining to the Chief Constable in late 1939, the parish council wrote, 'We consider the number of War Reserve Police employed in Ramsbury and district to be excessive'. However it must be remembered that the group also included officers from Aldbourne, Baydon, Chilton Foliat, Little Bedwyn and Froxfield, who collectively policed an area extending over 60 square miles.

To this force fell the responsibility of co-ordinating the work of the various Civil Defence services and as a result the organisations adopted the police district and divisional boundaries for their own areas of command.

Over the weekend of the 20th-22nd March 1942, Ramsbury police were involved in a very interesting exercise code-named 'Grim Jaunt'. The object of this was to train RAF air crew and cadets in escape and evasion from capture in enemy held territory.

A group of 150 RAF personnel (known as evaders) were dropped in pairs at various locations across Wiltshire. Their instructions were to avoid being captured and reach a pre-arranged rendezvous located about 25-30 miles from the dropping area.

S/C Mason S/C Brooks S/C Waight S/C Mills S/C Pike S/C Harrison S/C Tarrant S/C Gaskin S/C Baldwin S/C Reeve
S/C Ludlow S/C Duffield S/C Winchcombe PWR Nicholson PWR Groves PWR Chidsey PWR H/Pizzie
S/C Stanham S/C Blain
PWR Chivers Con Blake Sgt. Hurwood S/Sgt. Ray PWR Wells PWR Newton
S/C = Special Constable   PWR = Police War Reserve
The local police force pictured in the garden of Kennet House during 1941. (via P. Mills)

The defenders consisted of the Wiltshire Constabulary and approximately 200 RAF personnel, whose task was to find and capture as many evaders as possible. The Ramsbury section was assigned to strategic local positions: Whittonditch crossroads, Little Bedwyn railway bridge, the Lottage Road junction with Baydon Hill at Aldbourne and Stag Hill junction at Chilton Foliat. In addition officers were to patrol both Ramsbury and Aldbourne and to man public telephones. On spotting or capturing any evaders they were to contact Divisional HQ by telephone giving the operator the code-word 'Grim Jaunt' and asking for Marlborough 11.

The evaders were dressed in khaki denim battledress and were instructed to use all means possible to evade capture, short of criminal damage or violence. Unfortunately details of the outcome of this exercise were not recorded.

During the six years of World War Two the civilian population was constantly encouraged to report anything suspicious or unusual to the police. On 21st February 1944 a large number of thin aluminium foil strips were found around the village, and one was handed in to the police station. They were 10.5" long by 0.5" wide with a black coating on one side; the police duly passed these items on to Army Intelligence.

These foil strips, code-named 'Window', were top secret in 1944. They were designed to be dropped in large numbers by allied bomber aircraft, to confuse enemy radar by giving false echoes. Why these strips were found in this part of Wiltshire is unclear, however it seems most likely that a bundle was accidentally released during a training exercise.

The Ramsbury police contingent, like other Civil Defence organisations, worked long unsociable hours during the conflict. Fortunately they were never called upon to deal with any serious problems from either the Germans, the numerous British and foreign servicemen stationed in the area, or the civilian population. Nevertheless, by the war's end they could hold their heads up high at having maintained a high state of readiness to deal with any eventuality.

The Fire Service

By 1938 with war clouds gathering, the Government had instigated the formation of the Auxiliary Fire Service (AFS) whose personnel were all volunteers tasked to work alongside the regular Fire Brigades. It was during this period that Ramsbury set up its own AFS unit with Captain Ted Hill in charge. Shortage of cash forced them to construct their own fire engine by converting a Standard motor car and installing a pump in its boot. The vehicle was kept at what is now 34A the High Street.

One of Ronald Westall's duties as a 'runner' was to raise a crew should an incident occur at night. Captain Ted Hill would first be notified of the incident by telephone, and Ron would then to go to each of the volunteers' homes to wake the men up. This he did by simply opening each fireman's letterbox flap and shouting 'fire'. Ron had a list of all 12 personnel, and of these six were needed to man the pump. For the sake of fairness the six selected would be those who had not attended the previous call.

During the last week of June 1940 a new trailer pump was received that was designed to be towed by a private car. Although the village had recently installed new water mains and hydrants, there were still some outlying places that were not connected, and it was intended that they should be covered by this appliance. However considerable difficulties were encountered when using the road over Springs Hill, as the car was not powerful enough to pull the heavy new pump up the steep gradient. The pump was kept in a lean-to building (now the British Legion Club toilets) opposite the library in the High Street.

The AFS regularly held exercises, and on the afternoon of Sunday 22nd September 1940, they received a call to proceed to Lockeridge. It took them only 17 minutes to attend and they were congratulated on this achievement. It was also recorded in the same report that the men were still without uniforms; however by the beginning of 1941 each man in the unit had been issued with a dark blue boiler suit complete with AFS cloth badge, a tin hat, a gas mask and a pair of Wellington boots.

In addition to exercises and local fire duties, the AFS were often sent, during the winter of 1940-41, to support fire crews in blitzed towns and cities. Fully manned appliances from the surrounding area would gather at a convenient departure point before travelling in convoy on long unfamiliar journeys (made more difficult by the absence of road signs) to places such as Bristol, Southampton and Portsmouth.

In May 1941 the Government passed the Fire Service Bill, and in August the National Fire Service (NFS) came into existence. This absorbed the AFS and all the brigades formerly administered by local authorities, which were then re-organised into 50 area authorities spread across 12 regions. Ramsbury came within the boundaries of No. 39 Fire Force Area which encompassed the counties of Wiltshire and Gloucestershire.

All appliances were now painted grey and given their own individual code. Unfortunately the author has been unable to discover the code used at Ramsbury, however one or two unofficial documents suggest it may have been 39 – B – 6.

F. Westall   W. Jones   A. Westall   E. Kimber   A. Ponsford   A. Smith (Runner)
F. Smith   E. Brown   T. Hill   H. Marks
Other members of Ramsbury AFS not pictured above were: E. Westall, F. Barnard, G. Talmage,
S. Mundy and R. Westall – runner. (via P. Mills)

On Friday, 31st March 1944 the village witnessed its worst fire for more than 50 years. It started in one of the barns at Ramsbury Farm in Oxford Street (owned by Mr F.C. Giddings) and was caused by a backfiring lorry. This vehicle was normally used to collect waste from the military camps in the area. (Once all foreign material had been removed from the waste, it was turned in to a solid mass known as 'Wembley Pudding' and used as pig food).

The fire quickly spread to other barns and cart sheds before engulfing four cottages in Oxford Street and Chapel Lane. Ramsbury NFS was quickly on the scene followed by two American fire tenders from the airfield. These were then joined by appliances from Hungerford, Swindon, Marlborough, Bulford and Trowbridge. So great was the need for water to quench the flames that pumps and hoses were laid down to the river over 200 yards away. A detention party of Americans from the 101st Airborne Division had been working nearby when the fire started. One of the detainees escaped from his guards and helped put out the fire. It later transpired that he had formerly been a fireman in the United States.

The unfortunate residents who had lost their homes were initially cared for by neighbours, and furniture and belongings that had been saved were stored in nearby cottages and sheds.

The NFS remained in existence until 1948, and there were many who wished to see it continue as a nationalised body. However, when the NFS had been created, the government had given an undertaking to return all brigades to local authority control once hostilities ceased. Thus on 1st April 1948 the NFS was denationalised and Ramsbury's Fire Service became part of the Wiltshire Fire Brigade.

Ramsbury Platoon, C Company, 6th Marlborough Battalion, Wiltshire Home Guard.

Above: Ramsbury Platoon photographed at the school during 1944 (via J. Day).

Front Row *(left to right):*
R. Whitbread, G. Orchard, ? Watts, ? Sheppard, H. Watts, D. Huntley,
? Barrett, G. Chamberlain, W. Chamberlain

Second Row:
F. Starling, H. Palmer, H. Davis, G. Wilson, S. Smith, E. Wilson, J. Watts, A. Pike,
T. Peck, G. Edwards, W. Giddings, J. Claridge

Third Row:
A. Barrett, G. Claridge, ? Talmage, S. Mildenhall, ? Phillips, F. Hunter, F. Chamberlain, F. Wooton,
J. Isles, J. Sheppard, J. Dixon, F. Hunter, A. Exell, E. Watts, R. Rushen, ? Williams, M. Hughes,
A. Rosier, -?-, F. Newman, W. Parry, R. Lockey, L. Palmer, W. Dyer, E. Barrett, R. Dixon

Back Row:
E. Newman, W. Chamberlain, R. Griffin, ? Goodship, A. Wheeler, ? Blandford, ? Griffin, E. Hedges,
P. Westall, J. Day, E. Martin, ? Newman, ? Thomas, E. Martin, W. Grant

Ramsbury Platoon

This volunteer part-time unpaid army first came into existence on 14th May 1940, and was made up of men aged between 17 and 65. Its official title at this time was the Local Defence Volunteers (LDV) and by 17th May 50 men had registered in the Ramsbury section.

During the early stages no weapons or uniforms were available and the men trained with pitch forks and shot guns. However, this problem was partially eased when on 22nd May LDV commanders in Wiltshire and north Hampshire received a letter stating that rifles, ammunition, caps and overalls were to be distributed to all units in their area within 24 hours. The following morning the loading of four 3 ton lorries took place at the ordnance depot, Tidworth, and later that day one of these lorries delivered 80 rifles, 800 rounds of ammunition, 160 caps and 120 overalls to the armoury at Marlborough College. These items were then divided among the 523 volunteers of the Marlborough Battalion (which included the Ramsbury Platoon). A simple calculation shows that on average six men had to share one rifle.

At this time Ramsbury was a company area of Marlborough and Pewsey Battalion LDV and the Company organisation is shown below.

Company Area
Ramsbury

Commander
Capt. W. Brown, Manor House, Aldbourne

Platoons

No. 1 Ramsbury Platoon
Commander E. Wilson
Park Farm
Ramsbury

No. 2 Aldbourne Platoon
Commander Major S. Bland
The Warren
Aldbourne

No. 3 Baydon Platoon
Commander Col. Board
Baydon

No. 4 Chilton Foliat & Froxfield Platoon
Commander H.J. Skinner
River Cottage
Chilton Foliat

In August 1940, at the suggestion of Winston Churchill, the title of LDV was changed to Home Guard. The original 'Private Army' status of the Home Guard ended in November 1941 and the officers, who up until this point had no official rank, were given commissions in their respective grades. The full title of the Battalion was now No. 6 (Marlborough) Battalion, Wiltshire Home Guard. At about the same time it was made compulsory for men between the ages of 18 and 51 to serve 48 hours per month in either the Air Raid Wardens, the Fire Service, the Special Police or the Home Guard. The hours were relaxed somewhat during the latter stages of the war.

Ramsbury Home Guard platoon had a compliment of approximately 65 men. The old Wesleyan chapel in the High Street acted as headquarters and evening meetings were held there once a week. Lectures were given on Home Guard related subjects including, as one veteran recalls, "Making Molotov cocktails with petrol, a bottle and some rag." Every Sunday morning the platoon met on the football field (known locally as the 'horse race') for rifle drill, weapon maintenance and field movements.

On 7th December 1941, 25 of the men were receiving instruction in the art of grenade throwing at Barton Down, near Marlborough. In charge was Sgt.-Major Smith, a full-time Home Guard Instructor. Whilst in the act of throwing a live grenade, one volunteer hit his arm on the sand-bags surrounding the throwing pit and let go of the device. The grenade then bounced off the sand-bags and rolled down amongst other live bombs and detonators. Without a second thought Sgt.-Major Smith ran forward picked up the grenade and managed to throw it clear before it exploded.

Shooting practice was held two miles west of the village at an area known as South Side, near Axford. Most of the men would cycle to the range with their rifles slung over their backs, wearing full battledress and a heavy army great coat (this in itself was a major feat as many of the men were quite elderly). Initially the platoon had been equipped with the .303" Lee Enfield rifle. However towards the end of 1940 these weapons were withdrawn so that they could be re-issued to the regular army. The Lee Enfields were replaced with the Canadian Ross rifle which fired .300" ammunition. The Ross was a very accurate long barrelled weapon but was prone to jam with the smallest amount of dust.

'Tiny' Watts who lived at Balak Farm near Marridge Hill, and joined the LDV in 1940 at the age of 17, can clearly recall the Sunday that the platoon were issued with the Ross rifles. "We had to carry out some small skirmish movements in the water meadows, and whilst lying in a dry ditch I removed the bolt from the rifle, only to find that I couldn't replace it (kid with a new toy!). At this stage we moved on, so I put the bolt in my pocket. When we paraded for dismissal and the arms were 'inspected' nobody noticed. By the next parade I'd mastered it."

Later the platoon was issued with one Thompson sub-machine gun which was held by Sgt.-Major Smith. This weapon was fitted with a drum magazine and was identical to the 'Tommy guns' seen in American gangster movies which had enthralled British cinema goers before the war.

During the early days of the Platoon's existence the men patrolled the village in sections looking for parachutists, checking road movements and blackout infringements. The duty was additional to Sunday parades and was organised on a rotational basis, so that each member performed a patrol once every fortnight.

'Tiny' was in No. 4 section which also included Jack Watts, Walt Dyer and Harry Watts (no relation). After Sunday parades they would always adjourn to the Crown and Anchor to drink to Hitler's downfall. One Sunday after a few pints 'Tiny' recalls, "We went round to the downs behind Preston and put up some targets, all very unofficial. Ted Watts, Jack's brother, had got hold of a box of ammunition – I think he was the original Private Walker! We started to blast away gleefully at the targets only to have to abandon our fun and beat out the burning grass – all the ammunition was tracer!"

Frequent exercises were organised. They were usually held at weekends and often lasted all night. On one of these exercises 'Tiny' remembers defending a copse near Hilldrop. "Half the platoon was making a flanking move to attack us. We had acquired some blank cartridges (same source as the tracer) and as the attackers approached Harry Watts fired off a blank. At the same time one of the attackers, Wilf Chamberlain (who wasn't too good on his feet at the best of times), tripped on a bramble and fell flat on his face. Harry Watts jumped up, threw his rifle down and shouted 'I've shot 'im, I've shot 'im'. The management was not amused!"

During the summer of 1941 construction of the airfield began, and it was decided that the Home Guard should patrol the site which extended from Park Farm to Shag stile. The guard room was an outhouse at Park Farm which belonged to the Platoon's Commanding Officer, Lieutenant Ted Wilson. Four men would spend each night guarding the airfield on a 'two on two off' basis.

The hours of darkness in wartime Britain, where no stray light of any kind was allowed, were very dark indeed. On one of these nights, whilst guarding the airfield, 'Tiny' Watts fell over a sheep and recalls, "Unfortunately I was carrying my rifle more like the village poacher than one of His Majesty's soldiers and I ended up with some four inches of dust up the end of my rifle barrel. Some weeks later I walked into an open trench which caused Walt Dyer to fall about laughing, but by the time I'd recovered he had blundered into sheets of steel reinforcement mesh and was flapping about like a fly in a spiders web – last laugh to me!"

On Sunday, 15th February 1942 an anti-invasion exercise was carried out by the Home Guard and Civil Defence services, and it took the form of an imaginary attack by aircraft and paratroopers. Defensive positions had been built around the village at road junctions and other important points, and to add to the realism there were casualties, which were dealt with by First Aid teams.

Vivid memories of another exercise which took place over the weekend of 22nd-23rd July 1944 are recalled by John Day, who was then a 21 year old Private in the platoon. "The unit was split in two, one group was detailed to defend Marridge Hill House and the other had to attack and capture the property. Ted Watts and myself were members of the defending force and we were to keep watch on one of the roads leading to the house, and apprehend anyone using it. The only people we saw during the entire evening were two of the exercise umpires, whom we let pass without challenge (in our view the umpires were not part of the proceedings). After the exercise the platoon assembled at Marridge Hill to discuss the night's events, and the umpires expressed concern about how easily they had managed to approached the defended location. Ted Watts was very offended by these comments and told the umpires in no uncertain terms that they had been carefully watched and could have been shot at any time!"

This exercise finished at two a.m. and at six a.m. John Day had arranged to go on a flight in an American aircraft from Membury. He and three other weary members of the Home Guard cycled to the airfield where, to their surprise, they found the main gate unguarded. They carried on undeterred, and left their bicycles leaning against an airfield building. Some American personnel arrived on the scene and directed the group to a C-47 transport aircraft. Instead of a trip around the airfield which they had expected the four were flown to the ancient city of Edinburgh in Scotland where they were able to spend a few hours before returning home. After an exciting and trouble free trip the group, who were by now feeling very tired, arrived back at Membury. Here they experienced their only difficulty of the entire day. On reaching the main gate the sentry on duty there had no record of them entering the airfield and became very suspicious. There followed a long explanation which was eventually accepted by the guard, who then, grudgingly, allowed them on their way.

After D-Day the likelihood of the Home Guard being called into action became more remote, and in September 1944 attendance was made voluntary. In December the force had to stand down.

On Sunday, 3rd December a large contingent of Ramsbury Home Guard led by Lieutenant Wilson made the six mile journey to Marlborough to take part in the Stand-Down Parade in the High Street. Meanwhile Private Ted Watts was the sole representative from the unit to make the trip to London for its parade in Hyde Park followed by a concert at the Royal Albert Hall.

More than 50 years separate these two photographs. Above, Ramsbury Home Guard Platoon march past the Village Institute in the High Street, and below the scene as it appears today.
(top US Army, bottom author)

Aldbourne Platoon, 'C' Company, 6th (Marlborough) Battalion, Wiltshire Home Guard

Aldbourne Platoon photographed in the yard at Manor Farm. (via D. Barnes)

Front Row *(left to right):*
C. Dixon, W. Hale, L. Hawkins, E. Davis, W. Mayes, F. Wilson, W. Tilley, J. Barnes, T. Coles, H. Herring
Second Row:
G. Barnes, ? McHugh, C. Price, G. Dew, W. Liddiard, G. Sudds, Dr. Varvill, Cpt. Brown,
Maj. Bland, C. Brown, ? Mackeon, F. Barnes, ? Manning, G. Wooding, E. Pike
Third Row:
J. Morris, E. Avrey, J. Wilkins, H. Hamlen, J. Emberline, W. Jerram, J. Cuss, W. Liddiard, S. Holmes,
? Maskell, G. Wentworth, R. Read, F. Sheppard, F. Sheppard, G. Jerram,
Back Row:
D. Barnes, P. Haines, J. Roberts, W. Lee, J. Lee, T. Barrington, W. Sheppard, J. Bomford, W. Price,
T. Trotman, H. Aldridge, W. Hargreaves, F. Mildenhall, W. Barnes, A. Palmer, J. Mildenhall, H. Barrett

Aldbourne Platoon

The Band Room, near the village pump in West Street, acted as headquarters for Aldbourne Home Guard and the large open area around the pump was used for parades and drill. Bomb practice took place at New Barn, about a mile north west of the village along the Swindon road, and for rifle practice the platoon were driven by lorry or coach to Windmill Hill, near Lambourn.

Tommy Lunn was a Sergeant and Section Leader in the Aldbourne Platoon, and he owned a small garage and petrol filling station in West Street. From there he ran a vehicle hire service and owned a fleet of Ford V8 motor cars. Tommy offered the use of one of these vehicles for platoon duties. This was quickly accepted, and one car was suitably modified by applying a coat of camouflage paint and adding mountings for machine-guns.

The Aldbourne Platoon had a great variety of weapons at its disposal, many of which had been designed solely for use by the Home Guard. One such weapon was the Northover

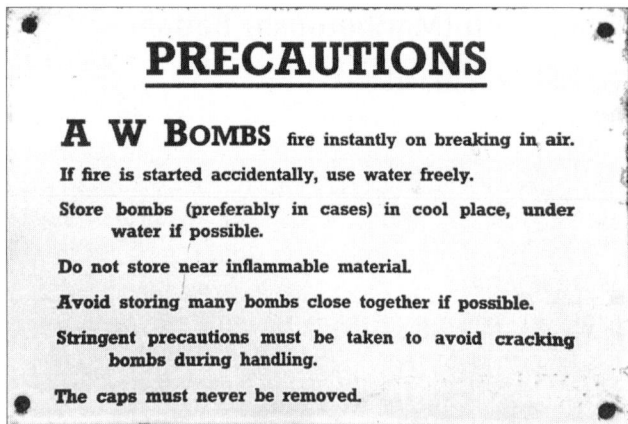

PRECAUTIONS

A W Bombs fire instantly on breaking in air.

If fire is started accidentally, use water freely.

Store bombs (preferably in cases) in cool place, under water if possible.

Do not store near inflammable material.

Avoid storing many bombs close together if possible.

Stringent precautions must be taken to avoid cracking bombs during handling.

The caps must never be removed.

(Left) Enamel plate entitled 'Precautions' found at Aldbourne. (Author's Collection)

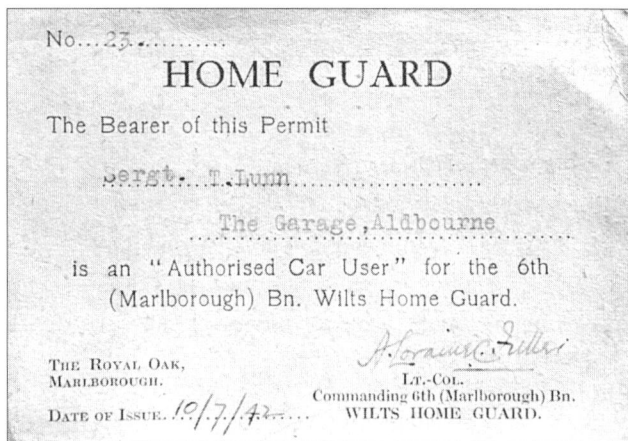

No... 23...

HOME GUARD

The Bearer of this Permit

Sergt. T. Lunn......

The Garage, Aldbourne......

is an "Authorised Car User" for the 6th (Marlborough) Bn. Wilts Home Guard.

THE ROYAL OAK,
MARLBOROUGH.   LT.-COL.
                              Commanding 6th (Marlborough) Bn.
DATE OF ISSUE. 10/7/42...   WILTS HOME GUARD.

(Left) The permit issued to Mr Lunn enabling him to buy petrol for Home Guard duties. This was signed by Marlborough Battalion Commander Lt. Col. A.L. Fuller. (Author's Collection)

Mr Lunn's camouflaged Ford V8 motor car pictured near the track leading to Four Barrows. Standing by the vehicle are, from left to right; Bill Price, Gerald Jerram, Les Stacey and Tommy Lunn. (Mrs M. Lunn)

A nice line-up of Mr Lunn's vehicles. The upstairs rooms of the building on the left of the picture were used as Platoon HQ. (Mrs M. Lunn)

Projector. This was a very simple and crude gun which derived its name from its inventor, Major Northover.

It could fire a number of different projectiles, but it was principally designed to fire the self igniting phosphorous grenade (SIP). This was a short-necked bottle of clear glass with a capacity of half a pint. Half of the filling was liquid phosphorous with the remainder being Naphtha or Benzene. Also included was a two inch strip of crude rubber. This was added to make the contents tacky, which in turn would make the liquid stick to the target against which the bottle broke. (These projectiles were also known as AW Bombs for the firm Albright and Wilson who manufactured the grenades).

Twenty-four of these grenades were packed into a wooden case, similar in design to a beer crate, which was provided with a lid. Screwed to the inside of the lid was an enamelled metal plate entitled 'precautions'.

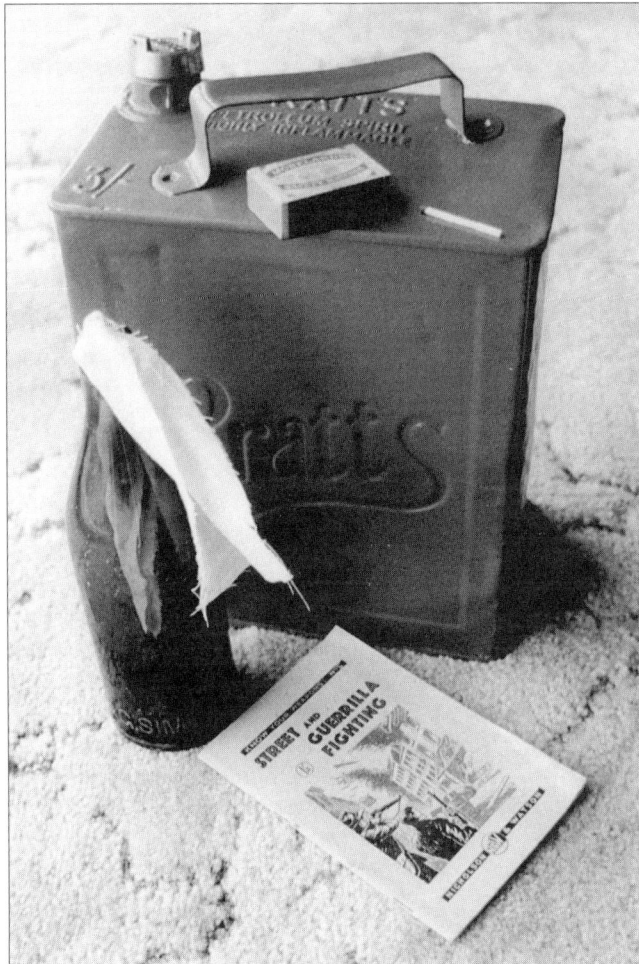

The 'Molotov Cocktail' – possibly the Home Guard's most famous weapon. It was designed to act as an anti-tank device and consisted of about a pint of inflammable liquid in a glass bottle. A piece of rag soaked in paraffin protruded from the neck and acted as a fuse. The weapon was crude and unpredictable and was often of more danger to its user than the enemy. (Author's collection).

Chilton Foliat Platoon, 'C' Company, 6th (Marlborough) Battalion, Wiltshire Home Guard

Chilton Foliat Platoon photographed in the grounds of the Old Rectory. (via Mrs M. Donovan)

Front Row *(left to right):*
H. Brooks, J. Bucknell, J. Watts, F. Lambourn, J. Povey, R. Rolfe, H. Denton, S. Cannings, -?-
Second Row:
E. Little, J. Bray, L. Hale, L. Rosier, J. Skinner, Capt. Brown*, T. Bucknell, F. Mundy,
T. Smith, R. Naish, A. Smith
Third Row:
F. Pett, A. Dixon, F. Bartter, A. Ball, S. Heath, A. Cooper, E. Williams, A. Pike, F. Hart,
F. Wooldridge, D. Smith, V. Little, A. Cannings
Back Row:
E. Lane, -?-, J. Dobson, D. Povey, S. Holmes, O. Dobson, J. Looker, G. Harrison, M. Roberts, F. Watts,
R. Copp

*Captain Brown was 'C' Company Commander, normally based in Aldbourne. To appear in this picture he must have been visiting or perhaps on an inspection tour.

Chilton Foliat Platoon

Headquarters of the Chilton Foliat Platoon was a first floor room at Mill House. Parades were held there every Sunday morning and Wednesday evening under the Command of Lieutenant Jack Skinner.

Most of the platoon were armed with rifles, except Lt. Skinner and one or two of the NCOs who had Sten Guns. Firing practice was held at the old chalk pit near Brickkiln Copse (now the site of the village sewer bed). There were two ranges, one used by the Army Cadets with their .22" rifles, and a longer range for the Home Guard who used .300" weapons (This range was often used by the United States Army during its time in the area).

Ronald Liddiard, then a young school boy living in the village, remembers a Home Guard demonstration on the Recreation Ground. An anti-tank gun (possibly a Spigot Mortar or PIAT) was loaded with a dummy projectile which was then fired diagonally across the field. Ron recalls that, "Everything seemed to happen in slow motion, and the bomb could be clearly seen as it was lobbed through the air from one corner of the field to the other."

Chilton Aircraft Home Guard Platoon

F. Edmonds   G. Shears   E. Edmonds   F. Holmes
V. Hanney   W. Treble   Bush (Commanding Officer)
Holmes   H. Aldsworth   W. Clark

The Chilton Aircraft Home Guard Platoon, pictured near the tennis court on the Chilton Estate.
(J. Bowes)

About a mile east of Chilton Foliat stands a large country mansion known as Chilton Lodge. In 1936 a small factory was established in the out-buildings behind the house. The firm known as Chilton Aircraft, designed and built the Chilton Monoplane, a small aircraft very much ahead of its time in design and performance.

The prototype first flew in 1937 and Chilton Monoplanes were to win a number of national and international races over the following 20 years.

The company built four production models plus parts for many more during 1938, and had nearly completed a second prototype for a larger, two-seater version when manufacture of private planes was halted with the outbreak of war.

Throughout the conflict Chilton Aircraft produced finished parts for various types of military aircraft, and like most factories engaged in the war effort, they had their own Home Guard unit whose role was to defend the factory in the event of an attack.

The Air Training Corps

In 1909 an association known as the Air League was formed. It consisted of a group of aviation minded citizens, who wished to see a proper air defence strategy adopted for the United Kingdom. During the 1930s the Air League sent lecturers up and down the country to draw people's attention to Britain's apparent lack of interest in military aviation. A move by the Air League, which attracted many air minded youngsters at this time, was the setting up of the Air Defence Cadet Corps (ADCC).

In January 1941, the Air Ministry recognised the value of this organisation when it created the Air Training Corps (ATC), whose structure was largely based on the ADCC. It was hoped that this organisation would provide a way of identifying suitable candidates for the Royal Air Force, before they became eligible for military service. The Corps was open to boys aged between 16 and 18, and within six months of its inception it boasted 200,000 members. Organisation was along the lines of the RAF, with the cadets being issued RAF uniforms and squadrons being formed on a regional basis throughout the country.

At first the Ramsbury lads who had joined 529 Squadron ATC, faced the prospect of a six mile cycle ride every time the squadron met at its base in Marlborough. However by January 1942 there were enough cadets in the village for a separate flight to be formed. In charge of this unit was the school headmaster Mr H.G. Ludlow, and not surprisingly the school served as Flight HQ. Here, with the assistance of Harry Marks and Steve Smith (a sergeant in the Home Guard), the youths were taught Morse code and the inevitable drill. Visits to operational airfields were arranged and in June 1942 the flight had the rare luxury of a choice of either Upavon or Boscombe Down.

The cadets soon discovered that the ATC uniform carried with it certain unofficial privileges. Many were able to enter Ramsbury airfield without a pass, where among other things, they were able to scrounge flights in aircraft almost at will.

John Starling, who joined the ATC during 1941, remembers that the flight rules were very simple. A qualified instructor had to be in charge of the aircraft and each cadet had to wear a parachute. The trips varied enormously. Some would simply be 'circuits and bumps' whilst others took the excited cadets further afield, to such places as the Marlborough Downs or Salisbury Plain. John can remember on one occasion flying over Fovant and seeing the regimental badges cut into the chalk hills nearby. On another occasion he recalls touching down at the emergency landing ground near Wanborough. His longest flight lasted about three hours and was a return trip to Liverpool.

The lads soon got to know many of the instructors, particularly those of 'S' Flight who dispersed their aircraft at the western end of the airfield near Park Farm. On 21st March John Starling and Wally Hurwood had a very lucky escape. Both cadets were looking forward to a flight in Oxford AB725 with instructor W/O Hazelton and pupil Sgt. Francis. However shortly before take-off they were told that passengers were not allowed on this training exercise, as the pupil would be performing some dangerous low flying manoeuvres. The pair were subsequently shocked to learn that AB725 crashed on that flight near Standlake in Oxfordshire, killing both the instructor and pupil.

Not every visit by the cadets to the airfield resulted in a flight. Sometimes they were given a chance to practice piloting in the Link Trainer. This ingenious training aid was a very basic representation of an aircraft, with cockpit controls and flight instruments. Two of these crude versions of today's flight simulators were kept in a hut on the instructional site. Nearby was a two storey building which housed the Bombing Teacher. The ground floor of this structure was painted white and the upper floor, representing an aircraft, was fitted with a bomb site and navigational equipment. A lamp projected a moving map on to the ground floor, and at the right moment the pupil would throw a switch, representing the bomb release. A few calculations would determine whether the drop was on target. Also located in this building was a Frazer Nash powered turret and projector for the training of air gunners.

Although the Airspeed Oxford was the principle aircraft seen on the airfield during 1943, other types appeared from time to time. It was not unusual to see the odd Avro Anson, and on one occasion the cadets witnessed the arrival of a Wellington bomber, which had been forced to land at Ramsbury following a technical problem. The cadets ran towards the Wellington, but were kept at a distance by RAF ground crew to prevent them examining the aircraft too closely.

Another Ramsbury cadet, Peter Ludlow (whose father was Flight Commander), can remember being sent on a week long training course to Torquay in Devon, where he stayed in the Grand Hotel on the sea front. The hotel acted as a receiving centre for would-be RAF aircrew. Here, on 10th April 1942, Peter successfully passed his course and was awarded the ATC Certificate of Proficiency Part 1, Pilot Training Syllabus. This allowed him to wear the much-coveted distinctive white flash on his ATC side cap.

Ramsbury airfield acted like a magnet to the local ATC cadets, and they were there at every available opportunity. Those belonging to 1866 Squadron, based in nearby Hungerford, were no different. This squadron was very popular with the young men of the town, and had a compliment of approximately 50. A number of these cadets had formed a band, whose base drummer was Don March.

From an early age, Don had been enthralled by aircraft and flying, and his main ambition was to become a pilot in the RAF. In early 1942 Don joined the ATC, and by the war's end he had amassed an amazing 350 hours flying time in 28 different types of aircraft – surely a record for any ATC cadet!

His first flight was from Harwell and had been officially organised by the ATC, but from then on his flying was very much the result of his own efforts.

Requests to fly, if respectfully made, were seldom refused and Don's first flight from Ramsbury occurred during September 1942. Here he managed to hitch a ride in an American C-47 from the 64th Troop Carrier Group. Don recalls, "I stood behind the pilot in the cockpit as we dropped at times to as low as 100 feet. I thought how marvellous it was and resolved to fly again whenever I could." Shortly afterwards Don had a further trip in a C-47 and was just beginning to get used to the Americans generosity when, quite suddenly during November, they departed. A brief period of inactivity followed, before the arrival in January 1943 of an RAF training unit (No 15 [P]AFU) with about 20 Airspeed Oxford aircraft.

Don's first flight in an Oxford was on 23rd January in aircraft serial no. P9094. "We entered via the rear port door and found the plane very uncluttered due to the lack of a turret. I sat behind the pilots and enjoyed a navigational flight which took us over the city of Oxford. I had a very good view as this type of aircraft was blessed with excellent cockpit visibility."

On 30th January, Don flew for the first time with Sergeant Adams, an instructor from New Zealand. Adams was a very experienced pilot whom Don felt would have been much happier on Operations. Don says, "Whenever we flew together, Sgt. Adams seemed to vent his fury by flying as low as possible – continuously! This trip gave me my first sight of Stonehenge, and we had to climb to go over it otherwise we would have knocked the whole lot down! We climbed slightly over Salisbury and then low once more as we passed Boscombe Down. When we landed Sgt. Adams knew that I had enjoyed it all tremendously and it was the first of many exciting trips with him."

Often the instructors would take aircraft up for test flights. Don says, "These were always great fun as it gave them an opportunity to let off steam. On 25th April I enjoyed three test flights with F/O Ryan at the controls. We engaged in mock dog-fights with other Oxfords which were also up on air tests. I have visions of Oxfords at odd angles just missing each other. Each flight lasted about 20 minutes."

What was perhaps Don's greatest claim to fame occurred on 12th July. He had watched the pilots carefully when they were up together, had read books on how to fly aircraft, and was convinced that he could do it! On this particular day he cycled with a friend to Membury and after several false starts 'borrowed' a Piper L-4 Cub, took-off in it, and completed a circuit. He thus became the only ATC cadet to solo an American aircraft in this country during World War Two. On his return to terra firma Don was greeted by a group of irate American officers and was very lucky to receive no more than a severe ticking off.

During the remainder of the war Don enjoyed numerous flights in a great variety of aircraft which took him across the length and breadth of the United Kingdom and (following the invasion) on to the continent. After the war Don, like many of his wartime ATC peers, finally realised his ambition and became a pilot in the RAF, after which he pursued a successful career in civil aviation.

(Right) The Link Trainer was the 1940s equivalent of todays computerised flight simulator, and was designed to give pupils elementary training in flying while on the ground. Each pupil at Ramsbury would have received several hours instruction on the Link Trainer, with particular emphasis placed on learning to fly by instruments only. This photograph was taken at Membury during 1943 by an American serviceman based there. (Col. R.A. Stone)

(Far right) Ramsbury's ATC Flight Commander, Mr. H.G. Ludlow. (P. Ludlow)

1866 Squadron ATC photographed at Hungerford Primary School, which acted as squadron HQ. Their C/O was Mr A.J. Chislett who is seated fourth from the right in the front row. To his left is F/Sgt. G. Howarth, an instructor from RAF Ramsbury, who was given the task one day a week of lecturing the cadets on various aspects of flying. Don March can also be seen; he's sixth from the right, second row from the back.
(Via D. March)

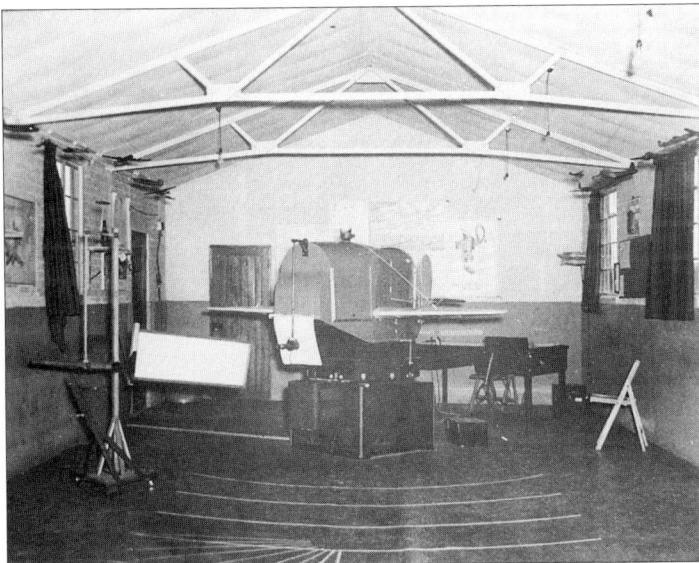

CHAPTER 2

LEND A HAND
ON THE LAND

Farming

The 20 years which followed the First World War witnessed a depressing decline in British agriculture, chiefly caused by cheap foreign imports. Many farmers eked a very modest living and bankruptcy was commonplace. The overall view of the countryside was of hardship and poverty.

Agriculture needed revitalising and the outbreak of war forced the government to act. War Agricultural Committees were created to give direction to farming activity. These 'War Ags' as they became known were organised on a nation-wide basis, the country being divided into districts, each with its own committee. They were given very considerable and wide-ranging powers. For example they could direct farmers to plough up grassland and instruct them to grow certain types of crop. Fines could be imposed on any farmer refusing to co-operate, and in very severe cases the farm could be confiscated and run directly by the 'War Ag' Committee. On the other hand, grants were available which encouraged farmers to follow government guidelines. One scheme allowed £2 per acre for ploughing up land which had been grassed for seven years or more.

By the end of the war Norman Day, a tenant farmer at Whittonditch, had reluctantly turned an extra 86 acres of land over to the plough. He was unhappy with this 'interference', as he called it, because in his opinion the farm needed every acre of its pasture for the dairy herd of approximately 20 cattle. The milk was collected daily from the farm in 10 gallon churns by the Milk Marketing Board and taken to Newbury. Another directive from the 'War Ag' required each farmer to increase his production of potatoes, and Norman allocated an additional two acres of land near the farmhouse for this purpose. The income from the sale of his harvest was very helpful, potatoes being sold to local villagers for 7/6d per cwt. In addition two or three pigs were kept in sties behind the stable. Each pig had to be registered with the 'War Ag' and Norman was allowed to slaughter one per year for family consumption. The remainder were sold at Newbury market.

Although farming was classified as a reserved occupation, many 'sons of the land' had volunteered for the armed Forces and this created a considerable shortage of labour. However the problem had been foreseen by the pre-war government who in April 1939 formed the Women's Land Army. These women came from many different backgrounds and walks of life. A considerable number had only ever lived in towns and cities and found country life very demanding. Nevertheless, once early teething troubles had been overcome the 'Land Girls', as they became known, were increasingly valued and many married local men and stayed on in the area after the war.

The extra effort necessary to increase food production was considerably hindered during the first winter of the war, which was the severest in living memory. In fact so bad were the weather conditions that the government declared it an official secret, for fear that the news could have been of use to the enemy. Mr P. Baldwin, head gardener to Sir Francis Burdett at Ramsbury Manor, recorded a temperature of seven degrees Fahrenheit (-14°C) on 21st January 1940! A week later a terrific ice storm which lasted for three days swept across southern England. Around Ramsbury, village pumps were frozen. Telegraph poles, electricity cables, trees, branches and fences collapsed under the weight of the ice and snow. Many roads were impassable, and birds were found frozen to trees! The severe conditions led to an accident in

(Right top & bottom)
During the long hot summer of 1940 in the clear blue skies of southern Britain the destiny of the free world was being decided. In the fields below, the farmers gathered in the first harvest of the war. Both photographs were taken near Ambrose Farm during August 1940. (W.C. Watts)

(Below)
The winter which preceded that glorious summer was one of the worst in living memory. Here Ambrose Farmhouse is seen deep in winter's grip. (W.C. Watts)

February between two vehicles near the top of Manor Hill. A bus heading towards the village lost control on the ice, hitting the kerb and skidding across the road. It collided with an oncoming school bus taking a group of girls to cookery classes in Marlborough. Fortunately there were no injuries. The intense cold and atrocious conditions continued throughout the month of February and well into March before the thaw eventually arrived.

The 'Lend a Hand on the Land' campaign was intended to encourage villagers normally employed as shop keepers, postmen etc. to work on the land in their spare time. Typical of these was Chris Winchcombe, a Ramsbury school teacher, who would often work on local farms after school hours and during his holidays.

Petrol rationing was introduced during the first month of the war, and the cutbacks had a dramatic impact on everyday life. Farmers were not exempt from these restrictions which made running their businesses very difficult. Fortunately most tractors were fuelled by a type of paraffin known as TVO, but in order to start the engine a small amount of petrol was required. In addition farmers frequently needed to get to local markets and agricultural merchants, which put extra pressure on their meagre fuel allowance. As a consequence they demanded, and were eventually given, extra petrol coupons.

The authorities soon realised that urgent action had to be taken to prevent such petrol allowances being diverted and used for private purposes. As a result all commercial petrol was coloured with a red dye. Police and Ministry of Transport officials were then given powers to stop motorists at any time and check for traces of red dye in their vehicle's fuel system. However it was not long before it was discovered that the colour could easily be removed by pouring the petrol through the filter of a gas mask!

After years of agricultural decline the war had at last reversed the trend, and by 1945 Britain's farmers were better equipped and more efficient than they had been at any time during the previous two and a half decades.

Prisoners of War

During 1941 a prisoner of war camp was established at Lodge Farm, a mile east of Baydon. It came under the control of Army Southern Command, later being transferred to South Midland Command, and was built to house 500 prisoners. It was designated as Camp No. 25.

When first opened the site held Italians captured during the early stages of the North African Campaign. It was classified as a labour camp for prisoners who had volunteered as agricultural workers, and thus provided a useful supply of manpower to local farmers. Labour was organised by the War Agricultural Committee, and the farmers paid for the prisoners services at a rate of 40 shillings a week for the first three months, and 48 shillings for every week thereafter. The prisoners in turn were paid a small amount between 6d and one shilling a day as pocket money.

POWs began to arrive in August 1941 and many were set to work in the fields nearby. After a short while some of the more trustworthy prisoners were billeted with local farmers. These farmers were all vetted by the Police in order to satisfy the authorities that they were honest and law-abiding citizens. Other prisoners were collected from the camp each morning by military vehicle and dropped off at their respective farms. At the end of the working day the vehicle would return to take them back to camp.

Some POWs were collected by the farmer in person. John Day can recall regularly visiting the camp, especially at threshing time, in order to collect Italians to work on his father's farm at Whittonditch. Advance notice was given to the authorities that labour was required and, when permission was granted, John would travel in the family car to the camp and return with two or three prisoners. If more were required, then his uncle would accompany him in another vehicle. Each evening it was their responsibility to return them all safely to the camp. He remembers on one occasion seeing a group of Italians stacking sheaves of wheat. Normally eight sheaves were placed in each stook, but these prisoners had not been instructed properly and were piling the sheaves into one enormous heap!

As the war progressed the Italian POWs who 'lived in' with a farmer were allowed a surprising amount of freedom. On Sundays they could attend a religious service unaccompanied if it was within three miles of their billet. If the distance was greater they had to be accompanied by a responsible person, and in these instances were allowed to use a bicycle. At the discretion of their employer they could take walks when not working so as long as they stayed within one mile of their billet. They were not, however, allowed to enter villages, towns, shops or any house other than that of their employer, and had to remain in their billets between sunset and sunrise.

In addition, as a security measure, prisoners were only allowed to post letters at the prisoner of war camp. They also had to carry an identity document at all times, and wear their distinctive uniform. This was identical in style to the British army battledress but was chocolate brown in colour with large circles of red material sewn onto the back of the jacket and the left trouser leg.

The employer also had to comply with certain conditions with regard to the prisoners' welfare. These included hours of work which were not to exceed those of any other employee, and each prisoner was entitled to one rest day a week, preferably a Sunday. The employer also had to provide suitable board and lodgings and three meals per day on the same scale as any other farm labourer who 'lived in.'

The Ministry of Supply (Home Grown Timber Dept.) made extensive use of POW labour. From late 1943 a gang of prisoners worked in Hens Wood, a large area of mature broad leaf woodland laying between the Kennet Valley and the A4 trunk road, south of Axford. With Britain's import of timber suspended, due to German occupation of the countries which normally supplied this raw material, much of Britain's woodland was felled for the war effort, and in this capacity it can be said that Hens Wood did its bit.

The prisoners involved in forestry work, like most employed in the area, came from Camp No. 25. They arrived each day by army lorry accompanied by an armed guard. Their arrival always caused the local forestry workers some amusement as they watched the guard hand his rifle to the prisoners before he jumped down from the lorry, the prisoners would then return his rifle before they got down.

The Italian POWs were experts at catching pheasants and rabbits, and regularly placed snares and traps in the hedgerows. The animals they caught would be prepared on site by a cook who always accompanied each group of prisoners. He would place the meat into a large cooking pot together with potatoes and other vegetables, which they brought with them, and create a savoury stew. The Italians found the grey squirrel to be particularly appetising, and if they disturbed one whilst clearing woodland they would all stop work to catch the unfortunate creature for their next meal.

As mentioned earlier, much of the timber was sent for war production and 'Harry' Williams from Axford, who was working for the Ministry of Supply at that time, remembers representatives from the Rotol Company visiting Hens Wood to select suitable Ash trees to use in the production of aeroplane propellers. The individual trees would be marked with the Company's name and a few days later one of their vehicles would arrive to collect them.

This cartoon by W.A. Sillince appeared on the pages of 'Punch' during 1943. (Reproduced with permission of Punch Ltd.)

"*Those are old Barleycorn's Italian prisoners busy digging for defeat.*"

An Italian POWs Story

Francesc Antonio Mazzotta was an Italian POW who, in common with many of his compatriots, remained in England after the war. His account begins in 1940 when at the age of 24 he was called up for War Service in the Italian Army. His peace-time occupation had been a butcher, although he spent most of his time in the army working as a baker.

After his training in Italy with No. 5 Compagnia Sussistcnza Regiment, he was sent to Libya, where in 1941 he was captured by the British. He spent some time in a prison camp in Egypt before being taken to India. He intensely disliked the conditions in India, and soon volunteered to work in England. Eventually, after a 31 day sea voyage he arrived on 27th February 1943 at Liverpool. After a couple of days he was moved to a prison camp at Lydiard, near Swindon, before finally arriving at Camp No. 25.

Francesc spent just over a year at Lodge Farm Camp, and for most of this time was kept busy erecting concrete posts, mainly beside railway lines. Initially the work was on the Lambourn Valley Railway, but was later extended to Newbury, Didcot, Abingdon, Uffington and finally Faringdon. Francesc was a Corporal Major (there were no Italian officers at the camp, the highest rank being sergeant) and was put in charge of sixteen other prisoners. They would travel six days a week (they had Sundays off) by army lorry to Lambourn station, where they were met by two railway employees. The whole group were then transported by train to their assigned place of work.

For each day's work they were paid the equivalent of one shilling in camp money, and were also allowed five cigarettes. Each barrack hut housed 12 inmates who slept in two-tier bunks. Their food rations included two loaves of bread per hut each day; however they often

Lodge Farm POW Compound (Camp No. 25)

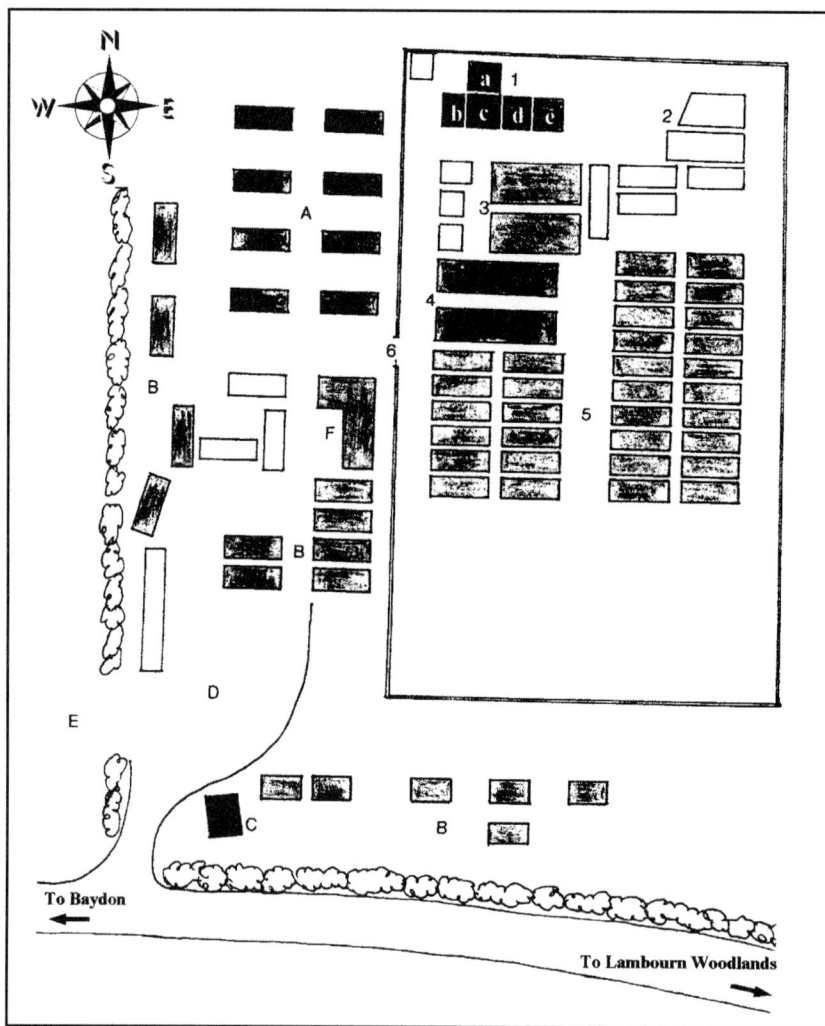

A = Stores and rations area
B = Accommodation for British soldiers
C = Officers club
D = Parking area for lorries
E = Prisoner overflow compound*
F = Office

* *This compound was used as an overflow area to accommodate Italian prisoners who had been moved out of the main camp in order to make way for the Germans.*

1 = Kitchen
  a) ?
  b) ?
  c) Room for cooking meals
  d) Workroom and dining room for cooks
  e) Butchers room
2 = Ablutions
3 = Dining area and theatre
4 = Sickbay
5 = Prisoner accommodation blocks
6 = Main gate

The areas between the huts in the main compound were cultivated by the prisoners for growing garden vegetables. This food supplemented and enriched their normal diet.

exchanged one of the loaves for a bag of flour, from which they made spaghetti. Some of the more skilled men had made a machine out of wood and other odds and ends to produce the spaghetti strands. In their spare time these men also made, from scrap material, items such as rings, clocks and cigarette holders. These trinkets were then sold, in many cases via the camp guards, to local people.

After his spell at Lodge Farm Camp Francesc was sent to work on a farm at Highworth, where he stayed on a 'live in' basis.

Generally the Italians were well liked by the locals, but they soon earned one universal attribute; they were experts at doing as little work as possible! Towards the end of the war the Italians left and their place was taken at Camp No. 25 by German POWs.

Life as a German POW at Camp 25

On 26th June 1945 Lodge Farm Camp was re-classified for use by German POWs. The few Italians that remained were kept in a separate compound in the south western corner. These Italians were regarded as potential troublemakers and as a precautionary measure were not repatriated with their fellow prisoners following the Italian surrender in 1943.

Heins (Henry) Fimmer was a German prisoner who, after his release from captivity, married an English girl and settled in Wiltshire. His story begins in 1943 when, at the age of 18, he was conscripted into the Wehrmacht (German army). After his initial training he was assigned to 4 Panzer Polizei Division, which was equipped with Panzer IV Tanks, and set off for North Africa. However the division only got as far as Greece before learning that the war in North Africa was over, and the Afrika Korps had retreated to Italy. Fimmer's unit remained in Greece for a while before being sent to the Eastern Front via the Balkans and Hungary, finally ending up at Danzig in north east Germany.

At this point in time they were completely cut off by the Russian army and their only escape route was across the Baltic in rafts which they constructed from wood and vehicle inner tubes. They managed to get as far as the island of Hela before being picked up by the Kriegsmarine (German Navy) who took them to the north German port of Stettin. Here they were each given a rifle and told that they were now in the Infantry! A train journey on flat open trucks followed which took them to Berlin. At this point Henry and two of his colleagues decided that they would try and break through the Russian lines and make for Hamburg which by now was in British hands. They succeeded in crossing the front line and were captured by the Americans. The date was 8th May 1945 and the war in Europe was over.

Henry and his compatriots were kept in farm buildings in northern Germany with nothing to keep them occupied until January 1946, when they were moved to a tented camp in Belgium. The conditions in this camp were intolerable. They were cold, underfed and overcrowded – 16 men living in tents designed to sleep eight!

At the end of March 1946 after ten months in captivity they were told that they were moving out. Many hoped that they would be sent home but to their dismay they found themselves being shipped to England.

Their destination was a transit camp at Bury St. Edmunds where their old German uniforms were exchanged for British battledress with coloured patches sewn on. One week was spent at this camp before a train journey which took them to Lambourn, and finally a short truck ride to Lodge Farm Camp.

The compound already held a large number of German inmates, most of whom had been captured in the Channel Islands. After the hardships that Henry and his colleagues had experienced on the Eastern front, they quite naturally felt some resentment towards these other Germans, who in their opinion, had had a 'cushy war' on the Channel Islands.

Prison accommodation consisted mainly of Nissen huts, each housing 27 inmates in two-tier bunks. All the prisoners at the camp were enlisted men except the camp doctor who was an Oberleutnant (1st Lieutenant).

Most of the prisoners worked on the land doing various jobs such as pulling sugar beet or turnips, picking potatoes or helping with the harvest, depending on the time of year. On one occasion after they had finished picking potatoes, the prisoners smuggled a sack on to the camp lorry. On the return journey the lorry passed through the village of Aldbourne where friendly locals warned them that police officers were searching the prison camp. Acting on this information the potatoes were quickly hidden beside the road and retrieved the following day.

On another occasion Henry Fimmer and his unit were sent to work at Froxfield pulling sugar beet. Working in the same field was a group of seven Land Girls. The Germans were in one corner and the girls in another. Henry says that he never saw two groups work so hard until they met in the middle! At the end of the day when it was time to go home the Land Girls' lorry had not arrived and it was decided that they should be taken back to their hostel in the POW vehicle. The British Guard, who normally rode alongside the driver, wanted to travel in the back of the lorry, but the girls hit him with their Wellington boots until he returned to the cab.

As already mentioned, many of the prisoners at the camp had been captured by the British following the liberation of the Channel Islands in May 1945. The following account has been compiled from a diary kept by one of these prisoners.

Wilhelm Straub was born on 5th November 1905 in the Bavarian city of Nurenberg, and was the eldest of three sons. Here, where the Nazis held their first rallies, he worked in one of the top hairdressing salons as a barber. He married his wife Berta in 1931 and their daughter (and only child) Irmgard, was born the following year.

In June 1940 Wilhelm was drafted into the services and after basic training was assigned to the Marine Artillery (a branch of the Kriegsmarine). Following a short stay at Wilhelmshaven he was transferred to France where he spent time at Calais, Boulogne, Le Havre and Cherbourg. After two years service in northern France Wilhelm's unit was sent to the Channel Island of Guernsey, where he worked as a barber and mail clerk.

Initially life on the island was uneventful. However following the Allied invasion of northern France in June 1944 things gradually began to deteriorate, and by January 1945 all mail and essential supplies ceased.

On 8th May 1945 the German garrisons on the Channel Islands surrendered. This presented the British with the problem of how to deal with an extra 26,000 prisoners of war, nearly 12,000 of whom were held on Guernsey. In the event the German POWs were sent to various camps dotted across the entire length and breadth of the UK.

On 16th May at 08:00 Wilhelm Straub and thousands of his compatriots were loaded aboard a 9,000 ton steamer berthed at St. Peter Port. The next day the steamer set sail for Southampton where it arrived the following morning. By noon the prisoners were on trains heading for Camp No. 23 at Devizes.

Wilhelm Straub's diary then reads, "On the morning of 26th June we were brought by train to Lambourn where we were put into tents. Our first excellent meal there consisted of mutton ragout, peas, boiled potatoes, pudding, cake and 'real' coffee." The final few months on Guernsey had left many Germans close to starvation and Wilhelm had become ill with a bleeding stomach ulcer. However, with the improvement in diet and care he received his ulcer soon healed.

The first few months in prison camp were not easy, there were repeated interrogations to identify the hard-core 'Nazis' and record what they had done during the war. The prisoners were often cold and wet and there was insufficient heat to dry out their clothing. However, as the weeks passed by things gradually began to improve.

To occupy their time the prisoners were encouraged to put on plays and Wilhelm volunteered to help with the make-up. The prisoners were also shown English and German films and allowed to participate in football matches. On 24th December 1945 the camp held a party where each prisoner was presented with a pack of tobacco and a Christmas cake. They were also provided with a very good dinner of baked ham, peas, potatoes and lots of cake. On Christmas Day the actors put on a stage performance.

Throughout Wilhelm's five-year military service he had been called upon to cut other sailors' hair. He was a barber in France, a barber in Guernsey and not surprisingly he became one of the camp barbers at Lodge Farm. In his view this trade was a blessing as he never went into combat, never had to use a weapon, was always indoors and usually managed to earn a little extra money.

His job frequently required him to travel to other local POW camps which were under the same administrative control as Camp No. 25. His journeys would often take him to Kingston Lisle, Faringdon, Challow and Marlborough. During these excursions Wilhelm came into contact with local people, many of whom lived on farms where they accommodated one or two prisoners on a 'live in' basis. Wilhelm would go to the farms to cut the prisoners' hair and in the process became friendly with the English families. On New Year's Day 1946 he was invited to dinner with the Wilkins family who lived near Faringdon. There they gave him a glass of beer which was a rare and precious thing for a prisoner.

After a further two years in captivity, Wilhelm was eventually told on 18th January 1948 that he was going home. In his diary he says, "Nobody can imagine the joy that I experienced upon the great news. I spent my last Sunday in Lambourn on 25th, and the weather was beautiful as I said goodbye to all my comrades. Our train left Lambourn for Newbury on 28th January and took us to Camp No. 43." (Harcourt Hill, near Oxford) One night was spent there before the train journey continued to Leicester where they stayed over night at Camp No. 4 (Scraptoft near Thornby, Leicestershire). The final leg of their passage across England ended at Harwich harbour where on 3rd February 1948 they set sail for Germany.

Wilhelm Straub's final entry in his diary reads, "I am sitting on my hammock writing these final sentences. We are full of anticipation and anxiety. The food is miserable but who cares, we are going home."

A Prison Guard's Story

In 1942, George Lang, a Scotsman from Glasgow, was called up for military service and joined 724 Company, Royal Army Service Corps (RASC). He landed in Normandy a short while after D-Day in June 1944. His unit was equipped with large Federal tank transporters and their job was to move equipment and supplies to and from the invasion beaches. The following months took George through France, Belgium, Holland, and finally, Germany. On his return to England George was posted to Bulford Camp, in Wiltshire, and at the beginning of 1946 was sent on RASC attachment to POW Camp No. 25. At this time he was promoted to Corporal, in charge of transport. Considering the number of inmates the size of the British security contingent was surprisingly small. They consisted of Major Raphel who was Adjutant, Captain Lynham (second in command) and approximately 14 other ranks.

Their motor vehicles comprised: Three 3 ton Bedford lorries,
Two 4 wheel drive 15 cwt Morris Commercials,
Two motorcycles, and two Staff Cars.

On the left Wilhelm Straub, wearing his naval uniform, poses for the camera on Guernsey during September 1942. On the right in a 1947 photograph, we see him as a POW in England. (Mrs I. Graham)

The only remaining building at what was once POW camp No. 25. This hut was positioned outside the main prison compound and may have been used as a store. (Author)

When George first arrived all repair and servicing of motor vehicles was undertaken at Abingdon, and it was not unusual for this work to take three months or more to complete, largely due to all the paperwork. Some of the POWs were trained motor fitters and George quickly made arrangements for them to regularly maintain the camps vehicles. They became very enthusiastic about the job and even constructed their own engine hoist. With the transport now being serviced on site the work was usually completed in less than a week. Every six months an army inspection team would visit the site to check on servicing standards. The vehicles were always found to be in excellent condition and Corporal Lang was repeatedly congratulated on these achievements. The prisoners who looked after the transport were normally excused roll call which, for all other POWs, took place three times a day during the morning, afternoon and evening.

Dances were organised fairly regularly, guests being invited from the surrounding villages. The music was provided by the prisoners themselves who had a very good ten-piece band. Sometimes the inmates were allowed out of the camp to attend local dances and Mrs Ludlow, from Aldbourne, remembers that they were always very polite and would click their heels before and after a dance. However, if a girl danced with a POW she would risk being ignored by the local boys for the rest of the evening!

Corporal George Lang T/14281728 (second from right) with some of the prisoners outside of the cookhouse at Lodge Farm Camp. (G. Lang)

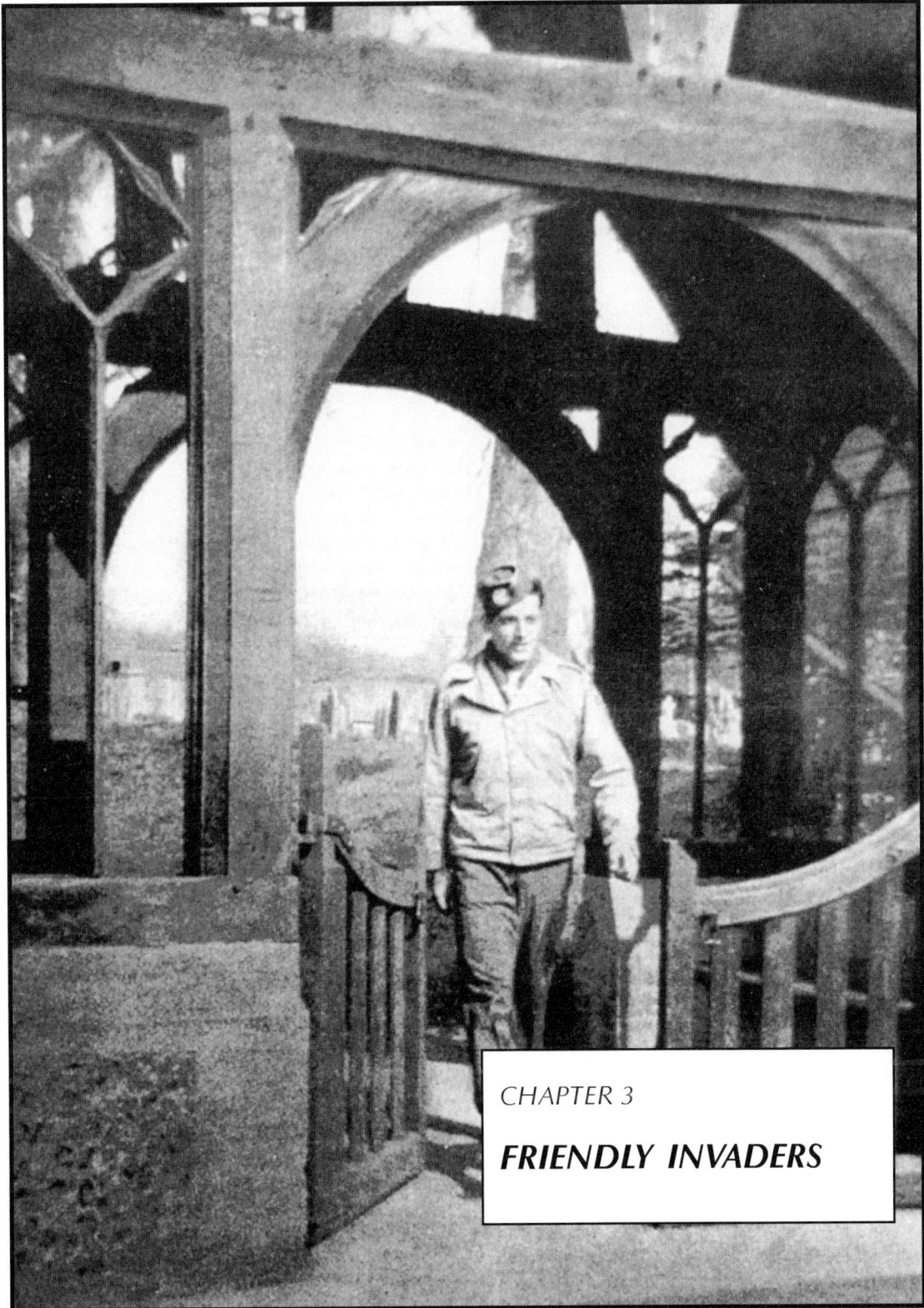

CHAPTER 3

FRIENDLY INVADERS

Worcester Terriers

During the six years of World War Two Ramsbury played host to many military units. The first to arrive was the 67th Field Regiment Royal Artillery, Territorial Army (affectionately known as the Worcester Terriers). The regiment was made up of two batteries, the 265th Worcester Battery and the 266th Malvern Battery, and on 1st September 1939, in the face of the increasing inevitability of war with Germany, these batteries were mobilised.

On 14th September the regiment left Worcester and Malvern in 'Midland Red' buses bound for Wiltshire. Regimental Headquarters and 266 Battery went to Ramsbury and 265 Battery to Aldbourne. The guns followed, towed by 1913 Commer lorries. This trip finished off these ancient vehicles and on arrival they all had to be scrapped and were replaced by Morris Quads (field artillery tractors). In addition to the Commers the regiment had a motley collection of commandeered civilian vehicles, which were also quickly replaced by new military transport collected from Newbury Racecourse. At this stage each battery consisted of three Troops, A, B and C in 265 Battery and D, E and F in 266 Battery, (A,B and C Troops were equipped with antiquated 18 pounder guns, some of which had been converted to 25 pounders, whilst D, E and F troops each possessed four 4.5" howitzers which fired a 35lb shell. These howitzers were also very ancient; two were dated 1898 while a third had entered service in 1912).

The regiment was part of the 48th Division (Western Command) which was building up strength in the Hungerford area. The Divisional formation sign (worn as a shoulder patch on uniforms and painted on to the mudguards of each vehicle) consisted of a dark blue oval in the centre of which was a blue macaw superimposed upon a red diamond. This emblem was introduced during late 1939 as a security measure. The macaw was chosen by General Thorne, 48th Divisional Commander, who was greeted on first entering his HQ at Littlecote by the words "Good luck, good luck" shouted by a pet macaw kept in the house.

The 67th's Regimental HQ was the Bell Hotel and their Commander, Lt. Col. Hobson, used one of the downstairs rooms as his office. Its bay window gave an excellent view of the High Street allowing him to keep a watchful eye on events outside.

266 Battery used the Crown and Anchor public house as its officers' mess, and the three Troops set up their individual headquarters nearby: D Troop at Parliament Piece, E Troop at Crowood House and F Troop at the Manor – the soldiers being billeted in stables, barns and private houses. Each troop consisted of three or four officers and 60 'other ranks', who were equipped with four guns and six Quads, two of which were used to haul the ammunition. These vehicles, along with all others of the battery, were kept in a large field behind Parliament Piece (later in the war this became the site of 'Camp Ramsbury'). When the new Quads first arrived at the Manor, Sir Francis Burdett who saw them coming up the drive, said with some relief, "Thank God we have got some armour". Little did he realise that these were 'soft skinned' vehicles which had no armoured protection whatsoever!

Training was conducted in stages, individual at first, then moving on to Battery, Regimental and finally Divisional levels. The regime consisted of gun drill, gas drill and route marches, signal training (held at the rear of Crowood House), and cross country runs. Being Territorial Army soldiers they had previously only worked together at weekends or on summer camps, and it was vitally important that they became fully integrated as a team as quickly as possible.

For live firing the batteries moved to a firing camp at Westdown, near Tilshead on Salisbury Plain, The Bustard Hotel being used as an offensive position during one of these exercises.

For recreation during weekday evenings, concerts, dancing and boxing were arranged in the Memorial Hall and at weekends rugby and soccer matches were organised. Every Sunday the batteries' wives and girlfriends were normally brought to Ramsbury in a bus operated by Mark's Coaches of Worcester, and this became known as the 'Passion Wagon'. Occasionally 'Pop' Reeves, a bus operator from the village, would conduct this trip which entailed a double journey to Worcester and back. Also on Sundays, officers from the battery were invited to tea with Sir Francis Burdett at the Manor. Each month everyone in the regiment received a 48 hour pass. On one occasion 2nd Lieutenants Malcolm Harding-Roberts and Tom Averill hired a car from the landlord of the Malt Shovel and managed to 'secure' some red dyed petrol. Whilst on their journey they passed a policeman on traffic duty. Although Tom Averill was annoyed that the officer had failed to salute as they went by, they decided not to stop and pursue the matter in-case he enquired about the petrol! On 18th December the entire Battery received ten days Christmas and embarkation leave, a good sign that their stay at Ramsbury was nearing its end.

After returning from leave preparations began for moving overseas. A few days before embarkation, the regiment was inspected by King George VI in Savernake Forest. The units were lined up in one of the forests many rides and then paraded past the King who took up position in a clearing. It was reported that the Monarch appeared gratified with what he saw.

On 7th January 1940 the vehicles and guns left for the port of Southampton. At dawn on 14th (exactly four months to the day after they had arrived) the remaining troops left for Hungerford station and boarded a train. Later that day they arrived at Southampton, where they embarked for Le Havre, to join the British Expeditionary Force (BEF) in France.

Shortly after their arrival the 67th Field Regiment were transferred to the 1st Division and moved to Belgium, where they remained until May 1940. Then, along with the remnants of the BEF, they retreated to France and were evacuated to England, along with approximately 330,000 other allied troops, via the beaches at Dunkirk.

Since the end of the war a number of the Regiment's veterans have made nostalgic return visits to Ramsbury in order to renew friendships and visit old haunts.

(Below left) Seen at Ramsbury during 1939 are, from left to right, Bill Palmer, Dennis Sweeting, Peter Sweeting and Cyril Palmer. The vehicle is a 15 cwt truck belonging to the 67th Field Regiment R.A. (C. Palmer)

(Right) Second Lieutenant Tom Averill photographed at Malvern during 1939. (T. Averill)

(Below) Men and machines of 266 Battery in Belgium during 1940. (S. Jones)

The Americans

The surprise attack by the Japanese on Pearl Harbor, in December 1941, finally brought the United States into the conflict. This was possibly the single most important event of the Second World War as it awoke the sleeping American giant and put the world's most powerful economy on to a total war footing.

American troops began arriving in Britain during January 1942, but it was August before this 'friendly invasion' descended upon Ramsbury, when the 64th Troop Carrier Group arrived at the airfield. Their stay in England was brief and tight security prevented any real contact with the local people. They departed in November and it was not until the following September that large numbers of Americans were again seen in and around the village. This time their arrival had a much greater impact upon the local population.

The units which were to spend the next nine months living and training in this corner of north east Wiltshire and west Berkshire were elements of the 101st Airborne Division – one of America's most elite, all volunteer parachute units.

As mentioned in an earlier chapter, the village population at the outbreak of war was approximately 1,500 so the abrupt arrival of 900 or so fit young men had a marked effect upon the area, which was further exacerbated in February 1944 by the arrival of the 437th Troop Carrier Group and its 2,300 personnel. In a matter of a few months the population of Ramsbury had grown by an astonishing 200%!

It had been anticipated by both the British and American Governments that problems would inevitably arise due to cultural differences, and considerable efforts were made to educate both sides in an attempt to avoid friction. On their arrival in Britain, American soldiers were issued with a small booklet entitled *A Short Guide to Great Britain* which outlined many of the contrasts between the two nations, such as language, money and customs. Most of the newcomers tried to be as pleasant as possible and were eventually accepted by the traditionally reserved British.

A very good example of how British attitudes mellowed is recalled by Ed Shames, who during the latter part of 1943 was a staff sergeant with the 101st Airborne Division. In November he was billeted with the Blain family, then proprietors of Hill's stores in the High Street. "I shared an upstairs bedroom with a colleague. The billeting officer who showed us to our room told us in no uncertain terms that the remainder of the house was strictly 'out of bounds'. Whenever we had a meal, or needed a shower, we had to go to the Memorial Hall or back to the battalion's camp in Love's Lane. For the first three weeks or so Mr and Mrs Blain kept their distance. Then one Saturday, while on leave, I went to Stonehenge (a surprisingly easy place to visit during the war, as there was a regular flow of military traffic from the camps in the Swindon area to Salisbury Plain). I returned to the village during the early afternoon and found Mr Blain busy working in his shop, which was inundated with customers. I asked him if he needed any assistance, adding that back home in Virginia I helped my mother run a small grocery store. My offer was cautiously accepted, and at the end of the day Mr Blain asked how much he owed me. I said that no reimbursement was necessary as 'Uncle Sam' was paying my wage, and that I would be delighted to help in the shop at any time in the future, providing of course I was not on duty. From that day on I could do no wrong. The following morning Mrs Blain brought me breakfast in bed, which included the rare luxury of a real egg. I was then allowed to use the Blain's personal bathroom facilities whenever I wished." As the weeks passed so their friendship grew and Ed kept in contact with Tommy Blain and his family for many years after the war.

Unfortunately, difficulties between soldiers and civilians still occurred from time to time. On one particular evening a GI, who was angry after being refused permission to enter The Bell, released a grenade in the square and fired a few rounds from his rifle. Children going to school the following morning were surprised to find bullet holes in Mr Marks shop, a small crater in the pavement at the front of Mr Pullens Antique Emporium, and the windows of the Windsor Castle public house blown in.

Approximately 10% of the American forces in the UK were coloured troops who were generally restricted to non-combat duties such as truck driving and construction work. The majority of the civilian population had never seen a coloured man before, but treated them with courtesy and respect which was greatly appreciated. However, coloured servicemen were segregated from their white colleagues and treated like second class citizens. Dance evenings, public houses, billets and even operational companies were allocated as either 'Black' or 'White'. At Marlborough for example the dances were open to 'White' GIs one week and 'Black' GIs the next. The 'Whites' would often ask the girls if they had been to a dance the previous week!

Build up to D-Day

From the early stages of the war Savernake Forest had been gradually transformed into one of the largest ammunition and bomb dumps in Britain, and in the weeks leading up to D-Day this storage area spilled out beyond the forest confines into the local lanes and byways. Around Aldbourne, in particular, an enormous supply dump was established. This contained small-arms ammunition in boxes along with shells, mortars, machine gun bullets and vast quantities of petrol in 'Jerrycans', none of which was kept under lock and key.

In addition to the troop concentrations and munitions stores already mentioned, other equipment of war was arriving in the area in ever increasing quantities. Both Ramsbury and Membury airfields had been allocated troop carrier and glider roles for D-Day, and during the late winter and early spring of 1944 transporters brought hundreds of large wooden crates containing dismantled gliders to the airfields for assembly. The crossroads at Whittonditch proved somewhat troublesome for the manoeuvring transporters, and on several occasions they knocked down the brick parapet of the bridge that carried the road over a small stream.

This crossroads also proved hazardous for the many convoys of tanks and trucks travelling south to the coast. Since the war the road layout in this area has been extensively modified. However in 1944 the main Swindon-Hungerford road veered left and then right at this point before returning on to its original course. The small stream which ran parallel to the road continued south at the point where the road veered to the east. Occasionally, on moonlit nights, truck drivers in these convoys would mistake the silvery stream as a continuation of the road and find themselves driving down the middle of it!

According to one local who in 1944 lived at Whittonditch, "The convoys seemed endless" and he remembers on one occasion trying to herd some cattle across the main road for milking. "It took half an hour for a gap to appear and as we started to move the cattle out of the field another convoy arrived, heading in the opposite direction!"

After D-Day many of the wounded were brought back to the nearby airfields. It was not uncommon, 20 minutes or so after aircraft had landed at Ramsbury, for convoys of American 4x4 Dodge ambulances to come racing down the hill from the airfield and head towards the American hospitals at Marlborough Common and Burdrop Park, near Swindon. The smell of ether wafting from the vehicles as they sped by is still vividly remembered by the same Whittonditch man.

On the evening of August 26th 1944 one of these ambulances, ironically carrying four wounded German POWs, was involved in an accident with an American military lorry about 400 yards north of Whittonditch on the A419. The ambulance overturned but fortunately none of the occupants suffered any further injury. Ambulances heading for Burdrop Park often stopped briefly in Aldbourne so that the local girls could say a few cheery words to their wounded passengers.

An aerial shot of the crossroads at Whittonditch taken shortly after the war. (Via J. Day)

101st Airborne Division

The division arrived in England by sea aboard two ships, the SS Samaria and the SS Strathnaver which docked at the port of Liverpool on 15th September and 18th October 1943 respectively. The 506th Parachute Infantry Regiment of this division left Liverpool on 16th September and travelled by train through the war-torn industrial Midlands to its camps in southern England. Some elements arrived via Hungerford station on the West of England Main Line, whilst others disembarked at Ogbourne St George, about three miles north of Marlborough. These units were then transported by trucks and buses to various camps in the area, which became the permanent living quarters for the regiment throughout its stay in England. C Company and the entire 3rd Battalion were assigned to Ramsbury.

The Division's training was conducted in the local fields and woods. The 506th Regiment often used Love's Copse, Pentico Wood and Aldbourne Gorse for this purpose. Robert Rader from E Company, based in Aldbourne, remembers making 'tail gate' jumps in Love's Copse and how they were often left there for several days, fending for themselves. He recalls the woods as being cold and damp places to stay and move about in, which they were expected to do regularly on squad, platoon and company size manoeuvres. Guy Wentworth, then a young child living at Ewin's Hill, remembers that these exercises would often involve the use of live ammunition. Human-shaped profiles made of brown coloured hardboard were positioned in hedgerows and used as targets. The laying of mines and detonation of explosives were also carried out in this area, as well as mass parachute drops. The 506th's first regimental exercise in England was held in this vicinity during October 1943. A month later the service company and regimental staff made a practice jump in Littlecote Park.

At about this time it was realised that certain key personnel in non parachute units would be needed as parachutists. To enable these men to qualify in this role, the 101st Parachute Jump School was set up on 21st October 1943 in the grounds of the 502nd Battalion area at Chilton Foliat Camp. Training began on 7th November and five qualifying jumps had to be made by each man. By June 1944, 400 men had qualified as parachutists at the school.

Jim Carter was a pilot with the 84th squadron of the 437th Troop Carrier Group in 1944, and remembers carrying trainee paratroopers during this period. "In most cases the paratroopers tried to get their five qualifying jumps in during the course of one day. The paratroopers would be dropped near Chilton Foliat and after landing a GI truck would take them back to the airfield. We would fly the aircraft back, pick them up again and repeat this process until they had all made their qualifying jumps. Most of the guys jumped willingly, however one or two would get scared when it was their turn, so the Jump Master would put his boot on to their rear-end and push them out! On one occasion a trooper became very hesitant and tried hanging on to the door frame. In his panic he grabbed the latch of the cargo door which swung open hitting the aircraft's fuselage and causing some damage. In the cockpit we did not know what had happened but we certainly felt that something was wrong. I sent the Crew Chief back to investigate and of course he told us that the cargo door was open. Fortunately the aircraft's controls were still working properly and we made a hasty landing. On another occasion, after the paratroopers had completed their final jump of the day, the Jump Master came up to the cockpit and told me he had a girlfriend living in Hungerford, and asked me to circle slowly around the edge of town so that he could jump out and visit her. This I did and as we flew back around I could see him gathering up his parachute and waving , indicating that he was OK."

Paratroopers ran a greater risk than the ordinary soldier of being cut off behind enemy lines. It therefore became apparent that they should be given instruction in skills which would help them live off the land, and local gamekeepers with their unrivalled knowledge in this area, were brought in to assist. Rabbits were caught in snares, fish stunned by dropping grenades into the river, and pheasants shot during the hours of darkness – the roosting birds being illuminated by light from a torch.

As D-Day approached so the exercises became more realistic. The 101st participated in three major exercises. The first was code named 'Beaver' and was held from 27th until 31st March at Slapton Sands in the South Hams area of Devon. This region had been chosen as it closely resembled the Utah beach landing zone in Normandy. The paratroopers were dropped randomly all over this part of Devon from the back of trucks ('tail-gate' jumps), as it was considered too dangerous to drop in to this area by parachute.

Back in Wiltshire a jump was made by the regimental demolition platoon on 17th April in Littlecote Park, where the platoon attacked a pillbox. This was a demonstration for the benefit of Brigadier-Generals Taylor and Howell who were watching.

The second exercise, code named 'Tiger', took place between 23rd and 30th April, again at Slapton Sands. This event gained some infamy as a result of an attack by German 'E' boats on a convoy of landing craft carrying assault troops – 946 American servicemen lost their lives in this action.

Littlecote was chosen as HQ for the 506th Regiment, and this photograph shows the Regimental Headquarters Company passing the house during a review. (J. Reeder)

The officers were given sleeping quarters in the house and used the Great Hall as their dining area. The man reading the paper was Captain Moon who was Regimental Communications Officer. (J. Reeder)

The final exercise, and the 101st's dress rehearsal, was code-named 'Eagle' and took place on the Lambourn Downs on 11th and 12th May – all of the D-Day departure airfields were used. Due to an error, planes carrying H Company of the 502nd dropped their parachutists around Ramsbury. The pilot of the lead plane had told his radio operator to check the Aldis Lamp and the rest of the formation mistook this for the signal to drop their paratroopers. A substantial number landed in Littlecote Park.

Men about to go into battle for the first time have many different ways of dealing with their emotions. Robert Webb, a Supply Sergeant billeted at the Bleeding Horse public house, felt a need to reacquaint himself with his maker. Accompanied by one or two of his colleagues he made his way to the parish church where the vicar talked for some time about the meaning of life. One thing that left a deep impression on the young Americans, was the revelation that 700 years earlier local soldiers leaving England for the crusades worshiped in the same church on the eve of their departure.

Soldiers going off to war try to take with them as much equipment as possible, and the paratroopers of the 506th were no exception. In order to allow men of the 101st to carry more kit the US High Command had looked into the possibility of using the British 'leg bag'. These bags were designed to carry a variety of equipment including radios, medical gear, machine gun tripods and extra ammunition. As their name suggests, they were attached to the soldiers leg. A quick release strap was operated just after the parachute opened and dropped the bag beneath the paratrooper on a 20 foot coiled rope, so that it hit the ground before the soldier.

To evaluate the use of these 'leg bags' a small number of 506th paratroopers were asked to perform a test jump. The group took off from Ramsbury airfield in a C-47 aircraft heading in an easterly direction. The plane turned through 180 degrees and flying very low, headed back towards the village. As it reached the west end the 506th paratroopers dropped from the aircraft and landed in an area now occupied by the village Sports Club. This was the first time the British 'leg bag' had been used by US airborne forces. The trial was judged a success and the bags were employed by the 101st on D-Day.

In the week leading up to D-Day the 101st were sent by truck and train to their departure airfields. The gliderborne elements of the 82nd Airborne Division, which had been based in Lincolnshire, moved south during this period so as to shorten the glider haul. Parts of this division were sent to Ramsbury airfield and promptly sealed into their barbed wire compound. Frank Guild, a Lieutenant serving with the 437th TCG, remembers the scene, "Since 23:00 hours men of the 82nd Airborne Division had been marching from their own area to the waiting gliders. As they came down through the camp loaded with equipment they sang as though it was just another practice manoeuvre." (See Appendix One for flight movement tables for both the 82nd and 101st Airborne Divisions).

The heroic deeds performed by the 101st in the days following 6th June are well documented but beyond the scope of this book. However on 10th July, after being in action in Normandy for nearly five weeks, the 101st was relieved and moved to a rest area near Utah beach. Over the following three days the division was shipped back to Southampton in landing craft and then on by train to their original camps and billets. Much publicity had surrounded the division's action in France and their return was greeted with enthusiasm by the local people. Robert Webb remembers that they were brought back in buses and the whole village appeared to turn out to meet them.

The 506th Regiment had suffered 983 casualties, including 231 men killed in action, and fresh troops were arriving from the United States to replace these losses.

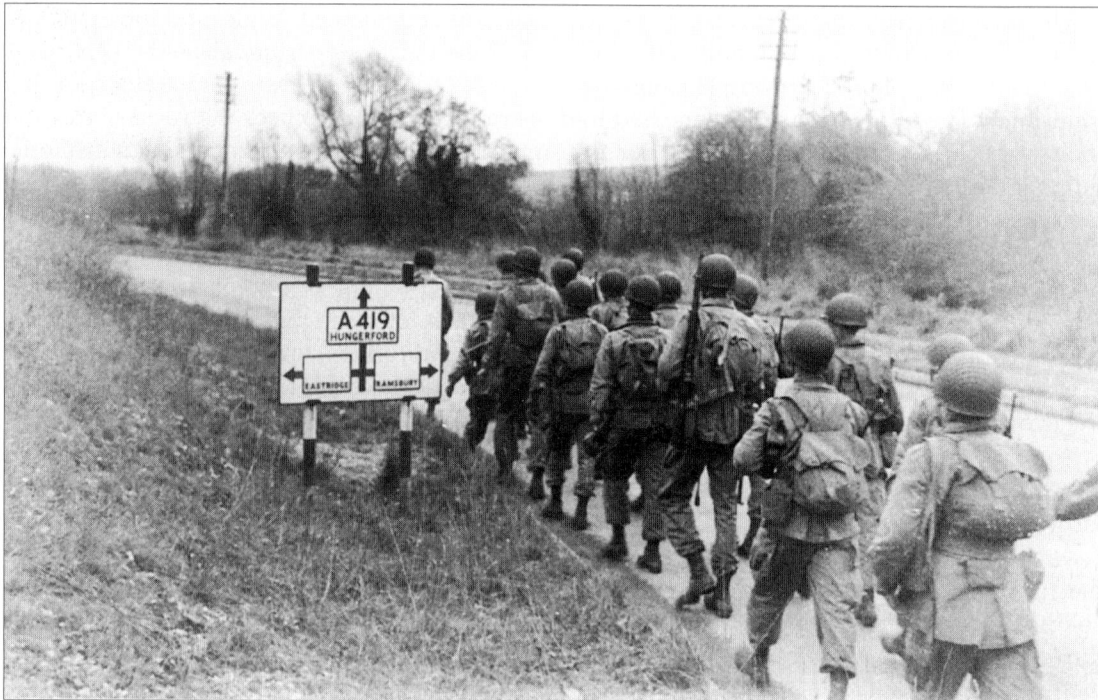

The lack of signposted roads totally confused the newly arrived American troops. Consequently the British authorities decided to replace most signs and name boards, as the likelihood of any German invasion was now considered remote. This view shows US Airborne troops on exercise approaching Knighton crossroads. (J. Reeder)

Occasionally exercises took place in Littlecote Park. This particular demonstration was performed on 17th April 1944 in front of Brigadier-Generals Taylor and Howell. (J. Reeder)

This Nissen hut was used by the 506th Regiment as their Red Cross club and PX (Post Exchange - similar to the British NAAFI). After the war the hut became Ramsbury's fire station and remained so until 1970, when it was demolished. The Wiltshire Fire Brigade then had a new station constructed on the same site. (Ramsbury Fire Brigade)

The down platform at Hungerford railway station photographed during late May 1944. The personnel, all from HQ Company 506th, were waiting for a train to take them to their D-Day marshalling area at Exeter airfield. The officer standing in the centre of the picture wearing a steel helmet was Col. Chase, the Regimental Executive Officer, and the Regiment's Commander, Col. Robert Sink, can be seen seated on the bench. (J. Reeder)

Further airborne operations were planned by the Supreme Command but, due to the rapid advance of the Allied armies across France, these were constantly being scrapped and replaced by new plans. Unfortunately this situation meant that the troops were kept at a high state of readiness and on several occasions were actually transported to their departure airfields. Of the operations planned, and subsequently aborted, the 101st featured in three code-named Transfigure, Linnet I and Linnet II.

Planning for Operation 'Market Garden' (the invasion of Holland) started immediately after Linnet II had been cancelled and was set for mid-September. As a result of the Allies' increasing air superiority the mission was scheduled to take place during daylight hours – a first for the 101st. The 506th Regiment's role was to secure the main bridge over the Wilhelmina Canal at Zon, then to push on south, take the city of Eindhoven and capture its four bridges over the Dommel River (See Appendix Two for the flight movement table for this plan).

The 506th Regiment's departure for Holland during September 1944 was to end the 101st Airborne Division's year-long association with Ramsbury. However over the past 50 years or so many veterans have returned on sentimental journeys to visit their old haunts and remember those who did not return.

US 101st Airborne Division Camps in England

Sept. 1943 – Sept. 1944

506th Regiment	**Littlecote House**	Regimental Command Post Regimental HQ Company HQ Company 1st Battalion Regimental Staff
	Ramsbury	HQ Company 3rd Battalion G Company 3rd Battalion H Company 3rd Battalion I Company 3rd Battalion C Company 1st Battalion
	Aldbourne	HQ Company 2nd Battalion A Company 1st Battalion B Company 1st Battalion D Company 2nd Battalion E Company 2nd Battalion F Company 2nd Battalion
	Froxfield	506th Service Company
	Chilton Foliat Camp	506th Parachute Maintenance Section
101st Parachute jump school	**Chilton Foliat Camp**	

502nd Regiment

Chilton Foliat Camp
- HQ Company 3rd Battalion
- G   Company 3rd Battalion
- H   Company 3rd Battalion
- I   Company 3rd Battalion
- HQ Company 1st Battalion
- A   Company 1st Battalion
- 502nd Service Company
- Regimental Command Post
- Regimental HQ Company
- Medical Detachment and Band

Denford Park Camp
- HQ Company 2nd Battalion
- D   Company 2nd Battalion
- E   Company 2nd Battalion
- F   Company 2nd Battalion
- B   Company 1st Battalion
- C   Company 1st Battalion

501st Regiment
- **Lambourn**
- **Hampstead Marshall – (tented camp)**

327th and 401st Regiments	Brock Barracks and Camp Ranikhet at Reading
377th and 907th Artillery Battalions	Newbury Racecourse
326th Medical Company	Donnington Castle (moving later to Templeton House and Standen Manor, near Hungerford)
101st Signals Company	Benham Park and Donnington Castle
321st Glider Artillery	Whatcombe Farm, near Great Shefford (in hutted camp)
326th Engineers and 81st Anti-Aircraft Battalions	Basildon Park, near Pangbourne
101st Divisional Command Post **101st Divisional HQ** **101st Divisional HQ Company**	Greenham Lodge

The story of Sergeant Gilbert Morton and his steel helmet

During the late 1960s when I became interested in the wartime history of Ramsbury, my aunt, Mrs Olive Winchcombe, gave me a rusty old American steel helmet which had been laying at the bottom of her garden at 27 High Street since 1944. She told me that it had originally belonged to a Sgt. Gilbert Morton of the 101st Airborne Division who had been billeted with her during the war. The helmet had a large dent on its right side, which probably explains why Sgt. Morton was allowed to give away this item of US government property.

I managed to trace Gilbert and found him living in retirement in the United States. The following account has been compiled from information kindly sent by him.

He arrived in England in late 1943 via the port of Liverpool and travelled with other units of the 101st Airborne Division by train and truck to Wiltshire. Here his unit, the 81mm Mortar Platoon of HQ Company, 3rd Battalion, 506th Parachute Infantry Regiment, were assigned to huts in 'Camp Ramsbury'. The camp, which had been especially built for the Americans, was in a field behind a large house in Back Lane known as 'Parliament Piece'. The house served as accommodation for officers of the regiment.

Gilbert Morton was 23 years old when he arrived at Ramsbury, was married with a baby son, and came from Illinois. He remembers the training being very strenuous but they usually had Sundays off when he was able to write letters home to his family.

About two months before D-Day some of the NCOs were billeted with local people in the village, and Gilbert's hosts were Mr and Mrs C. Winchcombe. He recalls, "I certainly enjoyed the change thanks to the warm family atmosphere at there home. Many times I remember taking Mrs Winchcombe a mess-tin full of sugar from the Army kitchen with which she would bake delicious cookies – sugar was a scarce commodity in wartime Britain." The Army kitchen was located in the former girl's school in Back Lane, recently redeveloped as private housing.

Opposite 27 High Street was the Village Hall where on most evenings films were shown or dances held. On one such occasion, when some coloured troops had joined in, a fight broke out, fortunately MPs quickly arrived and defused the situation.

Next door to Sgt. Morton's billet was the Congregational Chapel and every Sunday Protestant members of the Company attended religious services there.

About a week before D-Day the entire 3rd Battalion of the 506th Regiment was moved to Exeter airfield, and in the early hours of 6th June 1944, they parachuted into France. Gilbert Morton takes up the story, "When we jumped in to Normandy we were spread over a large area some miles from our objective. My plane load landed close to a wooded area where a group of Germans had made their camp. Four of us got together to try and find our way to the objective, which we later found was about three miles from where we had landed. We decided to follow a road we had found, thinking that we were going in the correct direction. At this point in time we did not recognise any landmarks.

I took the lead scout position with the others spread out behind me. We came to a crossroads where I crouched down trying to decide how to proceed. Across this dirt road I heard a noise and a German said 'Halt'. I hit the ground on my stomach, fired three times at him and he fell forward. I then jumped up and ran back down the road telling the others to follow. Before I reached the first man another German shouted 'Halt' and fired hitting my helmet – it stung so bad I thought I had a head wound. I was light headed for a few moments but thankfully the only thing damaged was my steel hat – it saved my life!

When we arrived back at Ramsbury I put the helmet on a post in your aunt and uncle's garden and told them that they could think of me when they looked at that old tin hat."

The rusty old helmet has now been in my possession for more than 30 years and forms the centre piece of my collection of World War Two memorabilia.

(Above) Sgt. Morton's steel helmet today. (Author)

(Left) Gilbert Morton in November 1942 during basic training at Camp Toccoa in the United States.   (G. Morton)

Many exercises were conducted in the area by the 101st Airborne Division. Here we see the communications platoon of the 506th Regiment on a 25 mile route march. (J. Reeder)

Camp Ramsbury 1943-1944

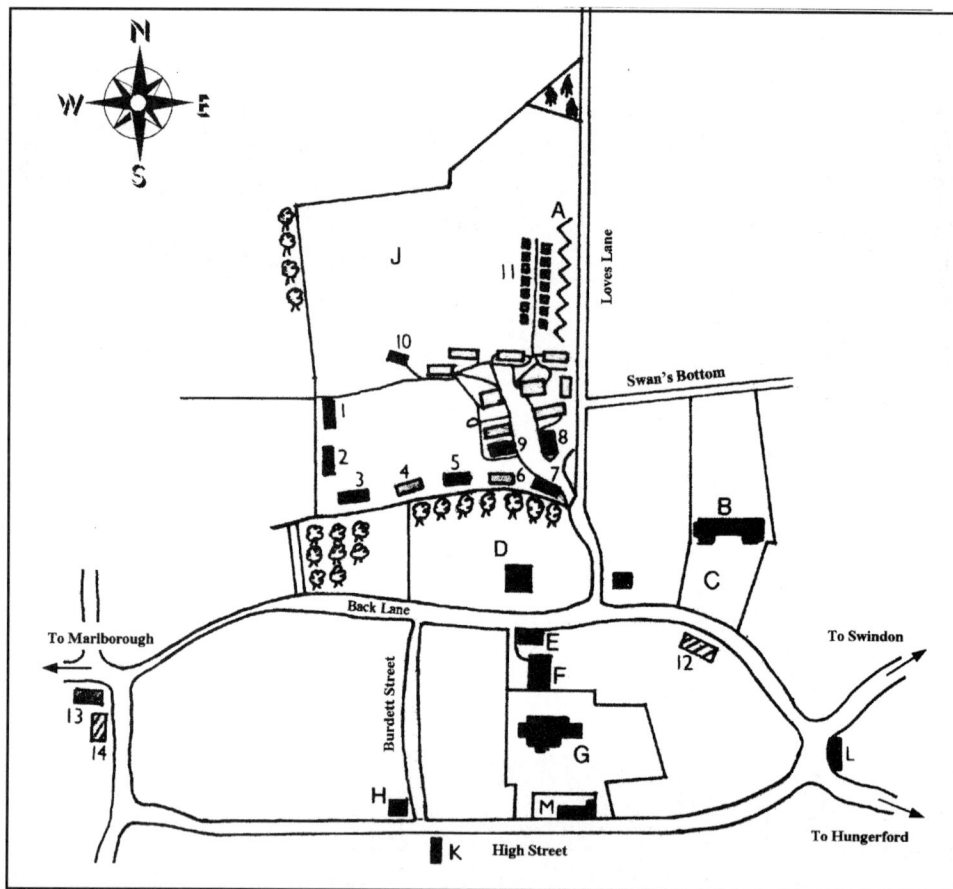

A = Air raid trenches	1 = Battalion sickbay
B = School	2 = Battalion dispensary and dentist
C = Playground used for German weapon training	3 = 81mm mortars
D = Parliament Piece - officer accommodation	4 = 81mm mortars and machine gun platoon
E = Church room - British Restaurant	5 = Machine gun platoon
F = Vicarage	6 = Communications (radio) supply
G = Church	7 = G, H and I Company HQ
H = Burdett Arms*	8 = 3rd Battalion HQ (CO Col. Wolverton)
J = Baseball and American Football pitches	9 = Latrine
K = PX (Nissen hut)	10 = Showers and washroom
L = Bell Hotel*	11 = Guard house
M = Village hall	12 = Mess hall and kitchen
	13 = Bleeding Horse* - supply Sgt's billet
* = Public house	14 = Barn used as store

Most of the remaining huts within the camp were used to accommodate men from G, H and I Companies. The 3rd Platoon from I Company was billeted at Crowood House, whilst the 1st Platoon moved in to the stables at the rear of the Bell Hotel. Company C from the 1st Battalion was sent to Ramsbury Manor where the men were accommodated in barns and stables.

Exercise 'Eagle', 10th-12th May 1944. Soldiers of Battery C, 377th Parachute Field Artillery, put on their parachutes before getting into their aircraft. Exercise 'Eagle' was the 101st Airborne Division's dress rehearsal for operation 'Overlord', and all departure airfields were those which the units would use on D-Day. Therefore this photograph was almost certainly taken at Membury.
(American National Archive. ref: 111- SC 293642)

Hungerford Common, 10th August 1944. General Eisenhower, the Allied Supreme Commander (centre left), pins the Distinguished Service Cross on 1st Lieutenant Walter G. Amerman of the 506th Parachute Infantry Regiment for bravery during action in Normandy. Also visible from left to right are: Major-General Maxwell D. Taylor, 101st Divisional Commander, and Major-General Lewis Brereton, commander of the US Ninth Air Force. Note the troops lined up in the background.
(American National Archive. ref: 111 - SC 424717)

At 11:00 hrs on the morning of Sunday, 27th August 1944 the 506th Regiment held a memorial service for the men killed in Normandy. It was conducted in the grounds of Littlecote Park with General Taylor and Colonel Sink presiding over the assembled troops from a reviewing stand decorated with parachutes. The service included an organ prelude, scripture reading, a flypast by a formation of C-47 aircraft and a reading of the roster of the dead and missing. 414 names were read out and to those present the list seemed endless. Shown here are; (Above) The reviewing stand with General Taylor and Colonel Sink at the front. (Below) Firing the salute for the dead and missing.
(Both photographs J. Reeder)

506th PARACHUTE INFANTRY
Colonel Robert F. Sink, Commanding
A.P.O. 472, United States Army.

Memorial Service
August 27, 1944
1100

Band Selection.
Organ Prelude.   "For Thee and all Thy mercies"   *J. Lancaster.*
    Private Jack W. Hayden.

Invitatory.

Invocation.

Orison.

Hymn   "America the Beautiful."

Scripture Reading.

Congregational Prayer.   "The 506th Parachute
    Infantry Prayer."

Vocal Solo.   "O rest in the Lord."
    Sergeant Donald R. G. Harms.

Address.   "Our heroic dead."
    Chaplain Tildon S. McGee.

Regimental Commander's Talk.
    Colonel Robert F. Sink.

Roster of our dead and missing.
    Captain Salve H. Matheson.

Firing of Salute.

Taps.

Band Selection.

"AMERICA THE BEAUTIFUL"

spacious skies, for amber waves of grain,
ntain majesties above the fruited plain !
ca, God shed His grace on thee,
rood with brotherhood from sea to shining sea.

lgrim feet whose stern, impassioned stress,
r freedom beat across the wilderness !
God mend thine every flaw,
self control, thy liberty in law.

es proved in liberating strife,
their country loved, and mercy more than life !
av God thy gold refine
leness, and every gain divine.

dream that sees, beyond the years,
leam undimmed by human tears !
shed His grace on thee,
h brotherhood from sea to shining sea.

HUTE INFANTRY PRAYER".

l to Thee and ask to be the instrument
evil forces that have visited death,
e people of the earth.   We humbly
e for all of our sins for which we do
orgiveness.   Help us to dedicate
Be with us, God, when we leap
abyss and descend in parachutes
ive us iron will and stark courage
s of our parachutes to seize arms
re many, Father ; Grace our arms
ame and in the name of freedom
m in our faith and resolution,
onor our high mission or fail in
s who have lived by the sword
rish by the sword.   Help us
nble in victory.   Amen.

Lt. James G. Morton).

A copy of the order of events for the memorial service held in Littlecote Park.

The Paras

Following the 101st Airborne Division's departure in September 1944, the village seemed comparatively quiet for a while. Gone was the regular sight of extrovert and energetic Americans 'jitterbugging' in the village hall or racing around the narrow village streets in their jeeps. The 437th TCG were still 'on the hill' flying re-supply missions to the continent, but in February 1945 they also departed. For the first time in more than two and a half years tranquillity descended upon the valley.

The villagers had little time to get acclimatised because in June 1945, following their return from the Mediterranean, the 2nd Independent Parachute Brigade was relocated in the area. The 6th Parachute Battalion (Royal Welsh) were sent to Lambourn, the 5th (Scottish) to Newbury, the 4th (Wessex) to Hungerford and the 2nd Parachute Squadron Royal Engineers to Ramsbury.

In charge of this squadron was Major Dennis Vernon MC. This officer's career had been distinguished and was particularly notable for the part he had played in the Bruneval raid of 27th February 1942. During this episode he led a team of sappers who successfully returned to England with components taken from the German radar station on the Normandy coast. These items allowed British scientists to unravel many German radar secrets.

To maintain moral it was considered important to keep the troops busy. Every morning at 08:00 hrs the squadron paraded on the school playground and during the day the men would be occupied with routine training, lectures and keeping fit. On the social side they could take part in soccer and rugby matches, as well as dances which were regularly held in the village hall.

The officers, like the Americans before them, were billeted in Parliament Piece and found their hostess, Mrs Wyndham, very charming. The remainder of the squadron was accommodated in 'Camp Ramsbury', and the Church Hall, which was only a short walk away, acted as squadron dining room.

Towards the end of October 1945 the unit was re-designated as the 1st Airborne Squadron Royal Engineers and prepared to join the 6th Airborne Division in Palestine. Not all personnel departed as many of them were awaiting demobilisation. This latter group continued to be known as the 2nd Parachute Squadron Royal Engineers, and were kept busy clearing up the camp.

Paratroopers are often considered by some to be a little reckless, and by others to be completely mad. In keeping with this reputation a plot was hatched, a few days before their departure, to blow up the old elm tree in the square. Fortunately the plan failed to materialise. However, during their last evening, the sentry box at the camp's main entrance was mysteriously destroyed by fire and some of the barrack buildings were damaged. The bill for repairs was reported to be £250, and each member of the squadron coughed up £1 compensation.

On 25th October the 1st Airborne Squadron decamped for Palestine and during the next 18 months saw Service in Iraq, Transjordan and the Sudan. By 1947 the British Army's task in the Middle East was drawing to a close, and its battalions began returning to the United Kingdom.

By the spring of 1946 RAF Ramsbury had ceased to be an active airfield, and languished on a 'care and maintenance' basis under the control of the War Department. The authorities soon realised that the site would make an excellent transit camp for troops returning from duty overseas.

In January 1947 the 6th Battalion (Royal Welsh) of the Parachute Regiment returned to England from Palestine. After docking at Southampton, they boarded trains for a two-day stop over in Blandford Forum. After some well-earned home leave, the troops were sent to various camps in the Swindon area. S Company found themselves at Ramsbury airfield.

HQ Troop of the 2nd Parachute Squadron Royal Engineers, photographed in the grounds of Parliament Piece towards the end of July 1945. Squadron CO, Major C.D.H. Vernon MC, is seated in the front row 6th from the left. (Via O. Atkins)

The machine gun platoon from S Company of the 6th Battalion (Royal Welsh) Parachute Regiment, seen posing for the unit photographer at Ramsbury airfield during the early months of 1947. (Via P. Baldwin)

S Company consisted of a Vickers machine gun platoon, mortar platoon and assault pioneers – approximately 200 men in all. Their duties during their stay were to assemble, clean and grease weapons before packing them into crates ready to be sent to Tidworth; the company's next base.

Peter 'Jake' Baldwin was a member of the company's Vickers machine gun platoon, and recalls very clearly his stay at Ramsbury. "The winter of early 1947 was extremely severe, everything was frozen and the place was thick with snow. We spent one day clearing snow from the Froxfield-Ramsbury road where drifts spread from hedgerow to hedgerow. Luckily, within a few days of our arrival, the thaw set in and we continued our duties in more pleasant conditions. We were billeted in black Nissen huts amid woodland where deer, pheasants and partridge roamed. The old gamekeeper had his lodge near us and would give the lads a couple of rabbits if he knew they were going home for the weekend. Wild flowers were abundant and I have never seen such large primroses. It was a delightful place."

S Company left after a stay of approximately nine weeks and went to Perham Down, near Tidworth, where they amalgamated with the 4th Battalion. Two months later the unit was disbanded and the troops demobilised.

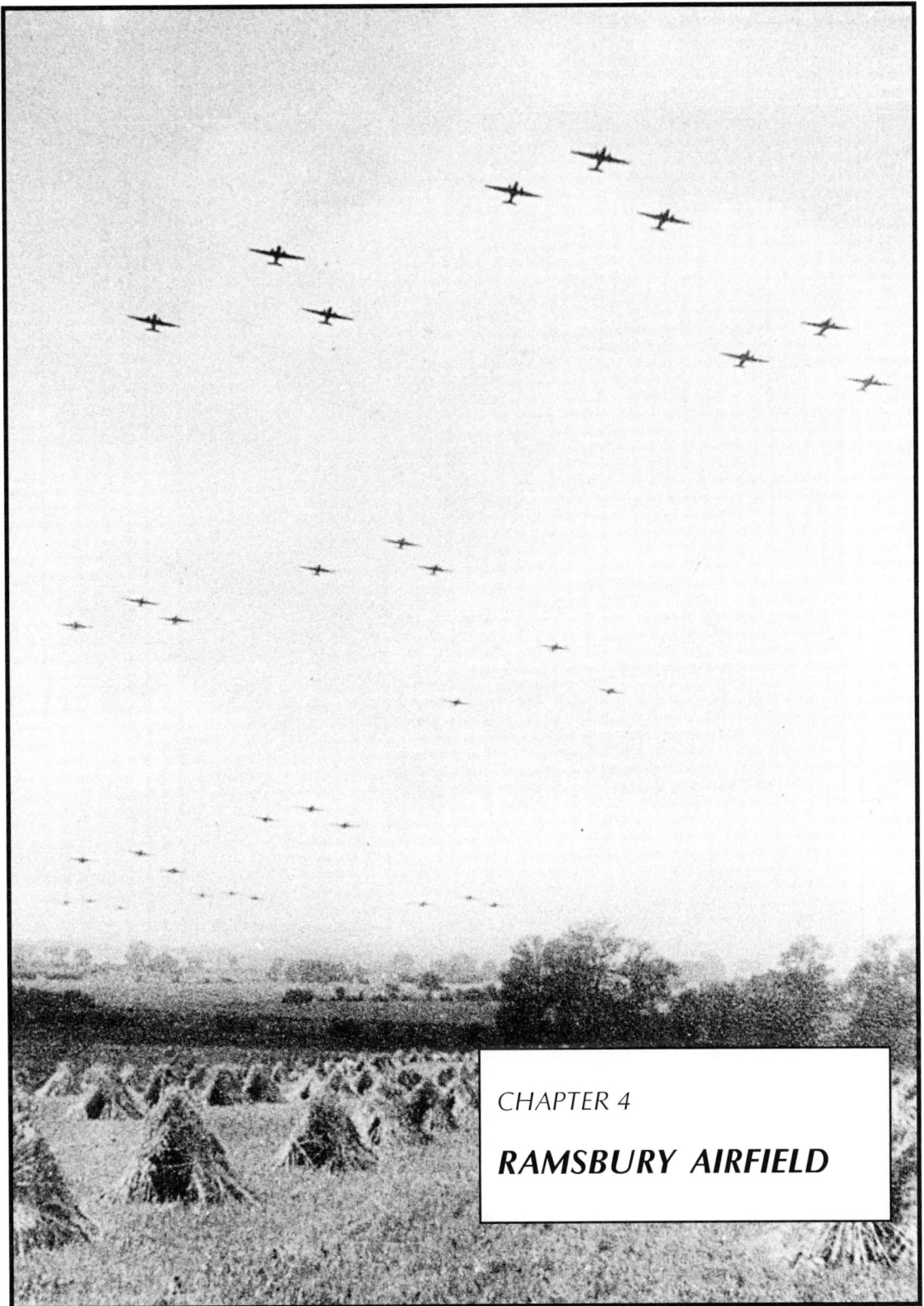

CHAPTER 4

RAMSBURY AIRFIELD

RAMSBURY - Location plan of airfield and dispersed sites

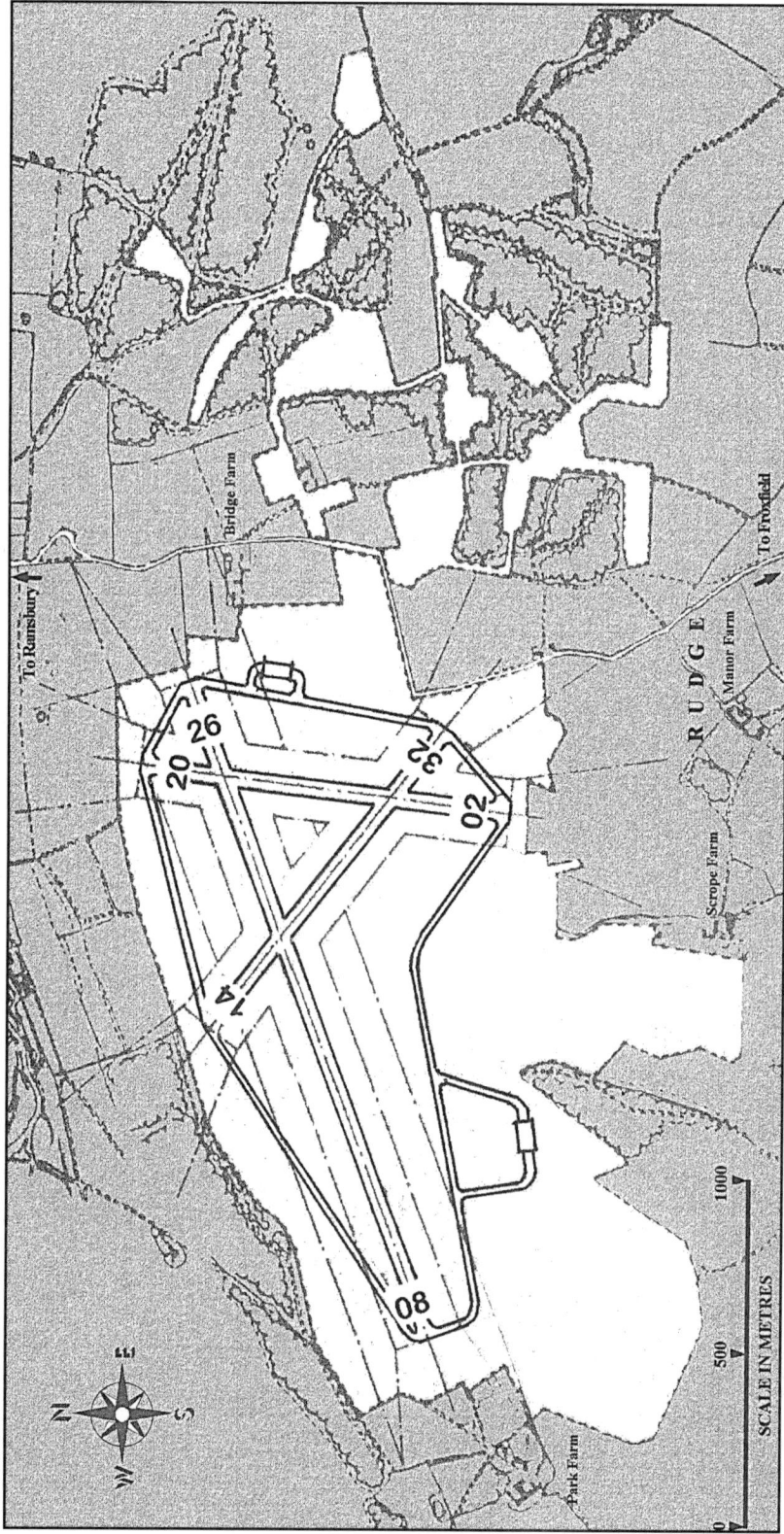

To Ramsbury

Bridge Farm

Park Farm

26
20
32
02
14
08

R U D G E

Scrope Farm

Manor Farm

To Froxfield

N
E
S
W
133

SCALE IN METRES
0   500   1000

Based on map of Ramsbury airfield (Drg. No 4958/44) held at RAF Museum, Hendon. © Crown copyright

The unshaded part of the map indicates the land controlled by the Ministry of Defence, and highlights the typical way wartime airfield living accommodation was scattered in surrounding woodland. This was a very sensible idea which, it was hoped, might reduce the number of casualties during an air raid. The numbers at the end of each runway correspond roughly to its compass bearing, divided by 10. Thus runway 26 represents a heading of 260 degrees from north. The number at the opposite end of the runway is, of course, the bearing in the other direction.

The Construction Phase

The site chosen by the Air Ministry for Ramsbury Airfield lies about half a mile south of the village, high upon the hill which dominates this part of the Kennet valley. In most respects it was an ideal location for an airfield.

Before construction work began the area had been composed of small fields bounded by hedgerows, interspersed here and there by areas of woodland; a scene unchanged for centuries. Fortunately only one or two unoccupied buildings had to be demolished.

Early in 1941 the land was requisitioned under the Emergency Powers (Defence) Act of 1939. In May a letter was received by the Parish Council from the Air Ministry, informing them of the closure of several public highways crossing the proposed site of the airfield at Elmdown. Construction commenced shortly afterwards and in the weeks that followed trees were felled and hedgerows bulldozed. With this completed, huge caterpillar earth movers arrived. Soon unfamiliar sounds echoed across the valley as work continued, day and night, scraping off the top soil and levelling out the fields in preparation for the laying of the runways and perimeter track.

The main contractor was Percy Trentham Limited of Dagenham, but much of the building work was sub contracted to local firms such as Wooldridge from Hungerford, and Downing, Rudman and Bent from Chippenham. The earthmoving equipment was supplied by Bowmaker Plant Company and the tarmac surfaces were laid by Tarslag. Many of the workmen came from the Irish Republic and one enterprising group used their spare time to distil illicit whiskey, selling the surplus to soldiers stationed nearby!

Bedford and Dodge three ton lorries were the most common types of vehicle used to bring the sand and gravel on site, and many of them were in a terrible state of repair. Anything that moved was pressed into service! Some of the lorries were driven by women of the ATS who would bring ballast from gravel pits as far afield as South Cerney, Theale, Burfield or Thatcham.

The completed airfield covered an area of approximately 500 acres and had cost the tax payer nearly a million pounds. Its plan followed the standard RAF Bomber Command pattern with three concrete runways each 50 yards wide, linked together by a perimeter track. The main runway, aligned with the prevailing wind, was 6,000 feet long and 33 aircraft hard stands were initially provided, later increased by the addition of a number of loop type dispersal areas. Two of the large T2-type hangars (the 'T' denoting transportable), 240 feet long and 120 feet wide were constructed, and living accommodation for about 2,400 personnel was erected in woodland to the east of the airfield.

The majority of runway construction work was completed in August 1942 when the airfield formally passed to No. 92 Group Bomber Command, who almost immediately handed over control to the Eighth USAAF. However many of the technical and accommodation sites were still incomplete and building work was to continue well into 1943.

The airfield during construction, showing an RD8 Caterpillar tractor pulling a scraper box. The driver was a Scotsman known as 'Sandy'. (Mrs R. Plenderleith)

The road in this 1937 photograph was removed by the contractors during the construction of Ramsbury airfield (W.C. Watts)

The same area as it appeared during the spring of 1995. (C.A. Day)

This photograph was taken during 1941 and shows the typical OTU runway layout beginning to take shape.
The River Kennet can be seen running across the middle of the picture
and the building visible top centre is Ramsbury Manor.
(Crown Copyright/MOD)

A civilian worker's story

One local man involved with Ramsbury airfield from the early days of its construction was Percy Luker. After leaving school in 1941 Percy went to work for Downing, Rudman and Bent, one of the many sub contractors used during construction of the airfield. His recollections provide an intriguing insight into those times. He recalls that at first the only buildings on site were the workmen's huts and a huge cement mixer, known as a Batcher Plant, placed near Burnt Wood. In the mouth of this monster all the cement for the runways was mixed.

When it became clear that the target completion date of early 1942 would not be met, the entire workforce was allowed unlimited overtime in a vain attempt to catch up. During the last few days of construction, every one on the site took a brush and painted the inside of all the huts with a yellow oil-bound distemper. Once the airfield was completed Percy was offered a civilian job by the Air Ministry and he remained at Ramsbury until 1945.

As the build-up to D-Day intensified so activity at the airfield increased, and at the beginning of June 1944 American paratroopers arrived. They were immediately moved into a tented and heavily-guarded barbed wire compound, hastily constructed in open space near the WAAF site. As part of other preparations made during this period, a tented hospital was erected by black troops of the US Engineer Corps in a field just south of the general mess site area. Fortunately, casualties in Normandy were fewer than anticipated, and it was never used.

Immediately before D–Day all movement on to or off the airfield was forbidden. Percy was 'imprisoned' on the site for almost a week, and he and his colleagues had to bed down wherever they could. Surprisingly, Percy managed to sleep through the entire events of the evening and early morning of 5th-6th June 1944 and was astonished when he awoke to find that all the troops and gliders had disappeared.

A few weeks later a group of German SS prisoners of war were brought back to Ramsbury from Normandy, and marched under close-escort through the camp to the cookhouse to be fed. Some of the American cooks working in the kitchens were of Polish extraction, and they became enraged at the sight of these much-hated symbols of nazi-ism. In Percy's opinion, had it not been for the guards, the prisoners would have been attacked and some would undoubtedly have been killed or seriously injured.

This page
All civilian workers employed at the airfield were given an identity card. The card shown below was issued on 20th July 1943 to Mr William Charles Giddings, who worked there as a groundsman.
(Mrs R. Penderleith)

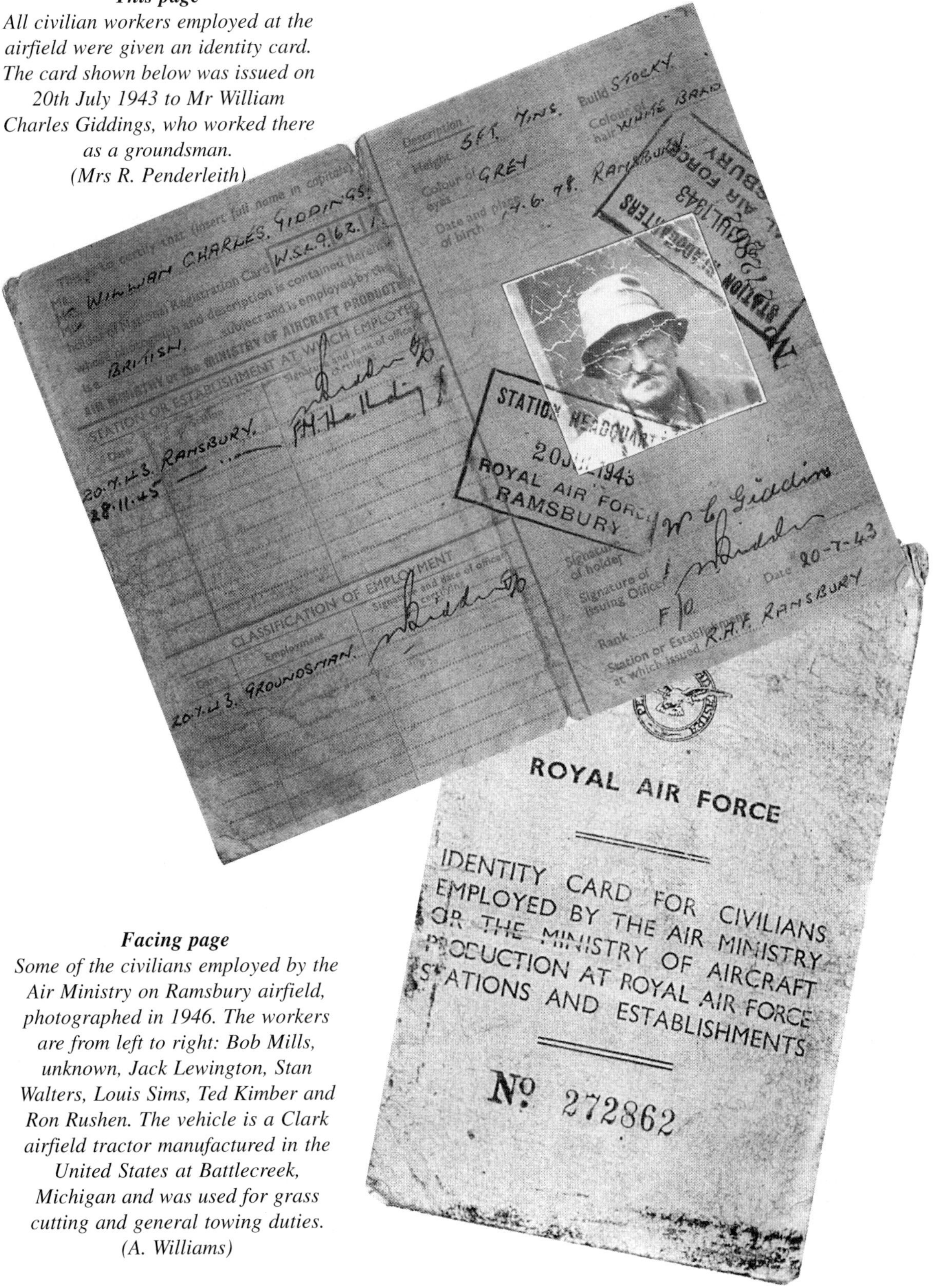

Facing page
Some of the civilians employed by the Air Ministry on Ramsbury airfield, photographed in 1946. The workers are from left to right: Bob Mills, unknown, Jack Lewington, Stan Walters, Louis Sims, Ted Kimber and Ron Rushen. The vehicle is a Clark airfield tractor manufactured in the United States at Battlecreek, Michigan and was used for grass cutting and general towing duties.
(A. Williams)

Airfield Lighting

Like most World War Two airfields, Ramsbury had an elaborate lighting system to guide aircraft on to the threshold of each runway during night landings.

This system consisted of an outer band of lights, approximately four miles in diameter, which encircled the entire airfield (a total length of some 12 miles). Leading off from this was a string of approach lights, mounted on poles 200 yards apart, which guided the aircraft into outer, intermediate and inner funnels. The outer funnel of lights was some 1,500 yards away from the threshold of each runway. The funnel lights were directed upwards and formed a 'V' shape, the sides of each being at a 45° angle to the centre line of the runway (See Fig. 1). These pole mountings were a source of irritation to farmers, as there were several hundred of them dotted all around the area, creating awkward obstructions in the surrounding fields.

As a navigation aid to pilots, most airfields featured an identification panel at each end of the main runway. The panels were built on a timber framework and formed 20 foot high illuminated letters displaying the airfield's two letter identification code (Ramsbury's were RY). These panels were located in Littlecote Park at the eastern end of the main runway, and in the west, behind a row of council houses called 'Kennet Rise' in the village of Axford. The lighting system was operated by a main control panel located in the airfield Control Tower.

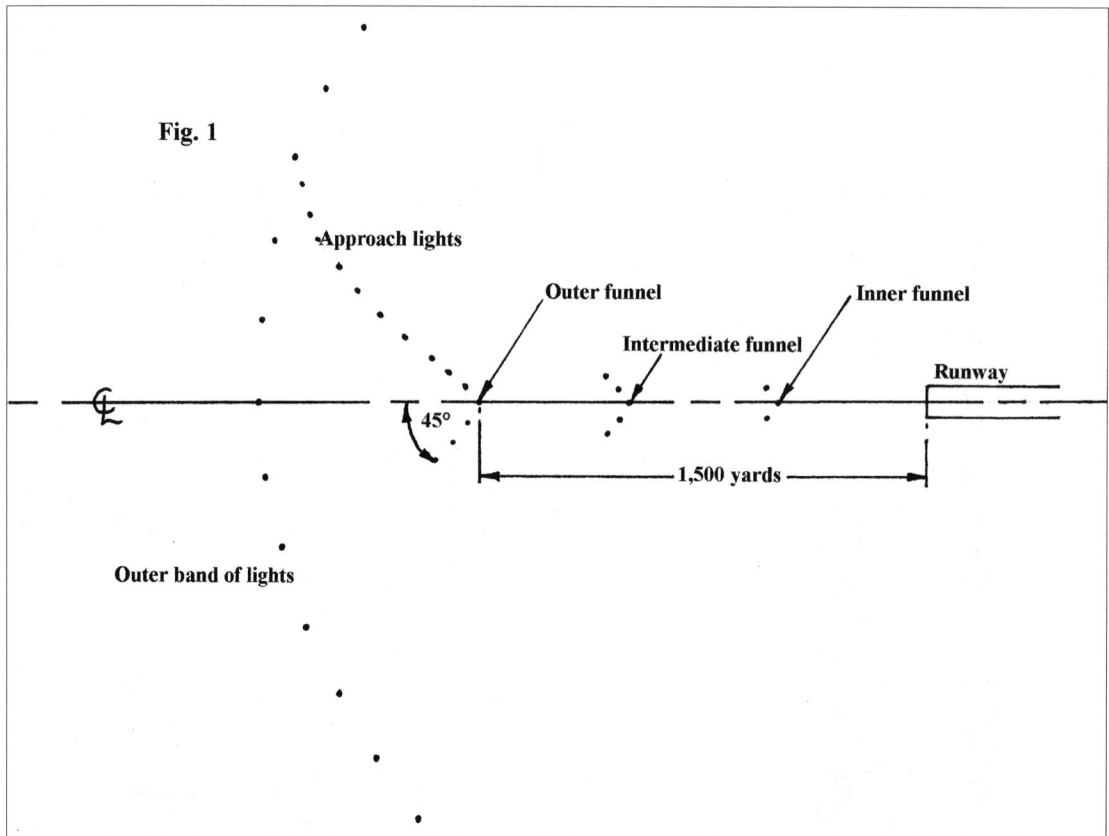

Fig. 1

Approach lights

Outer funnel

Inner funnel

Intermediate funnel

Runway

45°

1,500 yards

Outer band of lights

The Eighth USAAF arrive

Ramsbury was originally planned as an Operational Training Unit (OTU) airfield for Bomber Command. However the losses suffered by the RAF, bad though they were, were not as serious as had been feared. Therefore the need for OTU airfields was less urgent, and some of them could be considered for other purposes. As part of this revision, Ramsbury was earmarked for use by units of the United States Army Air Force (USAAF), which had started arriving in Britain early in 1942.

During August squadrons of the 64th Troop Carrier Group (TCG), a part of the 51st wing of the Eighth USAAF, began bringing their Douglas C-47 aircraft via Goosebay on the Labrador coast of Newfoundland into Britain. They flew across the Atlantic as part of the American military build up known as 'Operation Bolero' using the northern ferry route of Thule (Greenland), Reykjavik (Iceland), and Prestwick (Scotland).

On 23rd August they left Prestwick for Ramsbury. Unfortunately, shortly after take-off one of their aircraft crashed into a Scottish hillside. This was the Group's first casualty of the war and served as a grim warning of what was to come.

A week or so earlier the Group's ground echelon had arrived in England by ship at Liverpool, continuing their journey by train and truck. On arrival their first meal was provided by the RAF and consisted of bread, vegetables and a cold meat pie. One officer saved his pie for later as he thought it was his dessert!

The group had arrived in England earlier than had been originally planned, and long before the US supply organisation had been set up. As a result they were forced to live on British emergency rations for the first few weeks, which seemed to consist mainly of tea, biscuits, and orange marmalade. Some of the men became so hungry that they beat wheat out of the standing grain stalks and dug up potatoes from fields nearby.

The 64th's Commanding Officer was Colonel Tracey K. Dorsett, and the group was divided into four squadrons (16th, 17th, 18th and 35th). The aircraft were painted in olive drab on the upper surfaces and grey on all lower surfaces, with the individual aircraft identification letter in yellow on the rear fuselage. There were no group markings or squadron codes.

About two days after their arrival 'Lord Haw Haw', broadcasting on German radio, welcomed the 64th TCG to England and said that they would soon be dropping a calling card. Sure enough one night, about a week later, the Luftwaffe bombed Ramsbury airfield producing a few craters and wakening the personnel as the debris clattered down on to the metal roofs of their huts. Fortunately, the damage was minimal and there were no casualties.

Much of the 64th's brief time in England was spent ferrying supplies. Some trips took them to Liverpool, which was one of Britain's busiest ports, where huge quantities of equipment and supplies arrived from the United States. The city was ringed by a large barrage of anti-aircraft balloons and this made flying into its airfield a very hazardous business, particularly for the Americans who were unfamiliar with these obstacles.

Some training exercises also took place, which involved both British and American paratroopers. The American unit was the 2nd Battalion of the 503rd Parachute Infantry Regiment (PIR), commanded by Lt. Col. Edson Raff which had arrived in England during July 1942. The battalion was attached to the British 1st Airborne Division and billeted at Chilton Foliat.

Tight security during this early part of the war was paramount, and the 64th personnel were prohibited from travelling too far except for occasional trips to London. A deliberate deception plan was in operation, and speculation grew concerning the Group's first combat mission. This was fuelled by the issuing of summer and then winter clothing. All conjecture finally ended in

This August 1942 photograph shows an officer from the 64th TCG standing in front of a cottage in Scholards Lane, Ramsbury. (S. Harris)

American soldiers of the 503rd PIR prepare to board aircraft of the 64th TCG at Ramsbury during 1942. (US Army)

September when the 64th TCG was transferred to the Twelfth USAAF in preparation for its active involvement in operation 'Torch', the invasion of North Africa.

The group had 51 aircraft on hand at this time, all of which had been fitted with long range fuel tanks and exhaust flame dampers. During late October, the 64th TCG left Ramsbury to join other squadrons of the 51st Wing at the Cornish airfields of St. Eval and Predannack. Here the flight crews were briefed and the planes loaded with British and American paratroopers, in readiness for the first leg of their journey to Algeria.

On 9th November the group left England and made for Gibraltar. Two days later they set course for North Africa and after flying through a barrage of 'friendly fire' near Algiers the aircraft all landed safely at Maison Blanch. During the early hours of the following morning, with British paratroopers of the 3rd Battalion 1st Parachute Brigade on board, the group took-off and travelled about 200 miles eastwards to the drop zone near Bone on the Algerian coast. No enemy activity was encountered during the flight and every plane returned safely. The 51st Wing had played an important part in the success of operation 'Torch' and most of its' units remained in the Mediterranean Theatre for the duration of the war.

RAF pilot training

As the war progressed and Bomber Command's size and strength increased, the skies of Britain became too dangerous and overcrowded for inexperienced trainee pilots. As a consequence the Empire Air Training Scheme was conceived. Under this scheme future aircrew underwent their training in Canada, Australia, New Zealand, South Africa and Rhodesia. In these countries many thousands of wartime aircrew completed their service flying training, culminating in the presentation of their pilots 'Wings'.

Once qualified many of the pilots were sent to England to replace aircrew lost in the bombing offensive over Germany. These young men, accustomed to flying in clear blue skies with unlimited visibility, found difficulties in the crowded, murky skies of the UK. Special advanced flying units were formed to familiarise pilots with these conditions and No.15 (Pilot) Advanced Flying Unit (No.15[P]AFU) was one such school. Its original headquarters had been at RAF Leconfield in Yorkshire, but extra room was needed there to accommodate two operational bomber squadrons, and the training unit was moved to the less congested air space of southern England.

During December 1942 RAF Andover became the new headquarters for the greatly expanded No.15(P)AFU, with Ramsbury and Greenham Common allocated as satellite airfields for its Airspeed Oxford aircraft.

An advance party, consisting of HQ Squadron and some Maintenance Wing personnel, arrived at Hungerford station on 7th December. Their first task was to open up the airfield at Ramsbury, ready to receive other sections of the unit.

On the night of 15-16th December special trains carried the bulk of the unit's equipment and personnel from Beverley in Yorkshire to the rolling Wessex downland. 'S' Flight moved in to Ramsbury with its aircraft on the same day, their arrival being greeted by three consecutive days of rain. The first intake of 25 pupils arrived on 5th January 1943, when training began in earnest. Because suitable living quarters were unavailable at the other airfields, all WAAF personnel of the unit were initially sent to Ramsbury.

'Bill' Berry was an Australian pupil pilot who arrived on 26th April. 'Bill' (real name Ernest) had completed his initial flying training in Canada. After arriving in England he completed a British airspace familiarisation course at Worcester on Tiger Moths before moving on to Ramsbury. All of 'Bill's' flying up to this date had been on single-engined aircraft (Tiger Moths, Harvards and Yales) and he was assigned to No.15(P)AFU to convert to multi-engined aircraft, a prerequisite before moving on to Bomber Command. 'Bill' remembers what a pleasure it was to be able to taxi the Oxford without having to zigzag, as had previously been necessary in Tiger Moths and Harvards.

The airfield was still far from complete at this stage, with paths and roads unfinished and some buildings still under construction. 'Bill' says, "It was very easy to get an aircraft bogged down in the mud if you misjudged your position on the perimeter track, and I also remember how surprised I was to see women driving the big gravel trucks – something unheard-of in Australia."

Training consisted of 'circuits and bumps', single-engine flying, emergency procedures, day and night navigation exercises and instrument flying (with an instructor). 'Bill' remembers that one rather boring exercise was night 'beacon bashing'. "We would navigate our way around a number of red flashing beacons (these beacons, known as 'Pundits', flashed codes in Morse which identified the nearest airfield) eventually returning to our home base before starting the procedure all over again. If a pilot got lost he would call 'darky, darky' on the radio, and fly around a beacon giving out his own call sign. If the crew of the beacon were awake they would give him his course for home."

Unfortunately, training units and accidents go hand-in-hand. The first fatality occurred on 2nd March when Sgt. R.C.M. Webster (RNZAF) was carrying out a solo night flying practice in Oxford V3335. The aircraft collided with trees on the down-wind leg of a night circuit and crashed at 03:10 hrs. Another crash, involving Oxford AB725 from 'W' Flight, took place on 21st March and was officially described as an error of judgement whilst low flying. Both the flying instructor, Warrant Officer J.R.T. Hazelton and pupil Sgt. B.G.G. Francis perished. The remains of this pupil, an Australian, lie in a Commonwealth War Grave in Ramsbury churchyard. Ivan Cooke who was a fitter on 'W' Flight during 1943 was deeply saddened by the news of the instructor's death. "W/O 'Chiefy' Hazelton was an instructor on our Flight and I remember him well. He was a very experienced pilot who was highly regarded by all who knew him, and the majority of the ground crew were unwilling to accept that he may have been flying the aircraft when it crashed. He had already completed one tour of operations and it seemed ironic that he should lose his life over the relatively peaceful countryside of southern England."

On 7th June Oxford R6388 dived into the ground near the village killing the pilot Ken Deacon. 'Bill' Berry was on the same course as Ken and remembers him well. "The crash had been observed by another pilot who said that he just appeared to go straight in from about 3,000 ft. with no apparent flying difficulties, just as though he had suffered a heart attack."

Until the end of May Ramsbury had been classified as an 'army co-operation command aerodrome', but this command closed down on the 31st and the following day it became a training command station.

Intensive training of new aircrew meant that considerable aerial activity took place both day and night, and when additional Flights arrived during late July activity increased further. The Flights, previously based at Grove near Wantage, were obliged to move out to make room for elements of the Ninth USAAF. The removal of most of the unit's equipment was undertaken by using their own Oxford aircraft, and Australian Tom Parsons (then an instructor with No.15(P)AFU), remembers making four trips between Grove and Ramsbury. "Various items were stacked into the aircraft after the pilot had gone up front, and the plane was loaded to its maximum which made take-off somewhat hazardous. Only the very bulky and heavy items went by road."

The unit often used nearby Membury airfield for night flying instruction as Tom recalls, "The Americans had an operational unit there (67th Reconnaissance Group, Eighth USAAF) and one night F/O Marsden and myself went over with 10 pupils and four Oxfords to fly the night's detail. An American officer and two girls came up in a Jeep to watch us, then at 01:30 hrs they brought us a supper consisting of lobster, salad, fruit salad, cakes and Coka-Cola. We had a good feed and in return took them for a flight around the circuit."

George Reid, another instructor at Ramsbury, was also sent to Membury during this period but for a very different reason. "I was detached to the Yanks at Membury to help convert a squadron of Civil Air Guard pilots from single engine fighters to A20s, or 'Bostons' as we called them. They were from Texas and all seemed to be millionaires who were completely mad. They were amongst the first Yanks to be blooded."

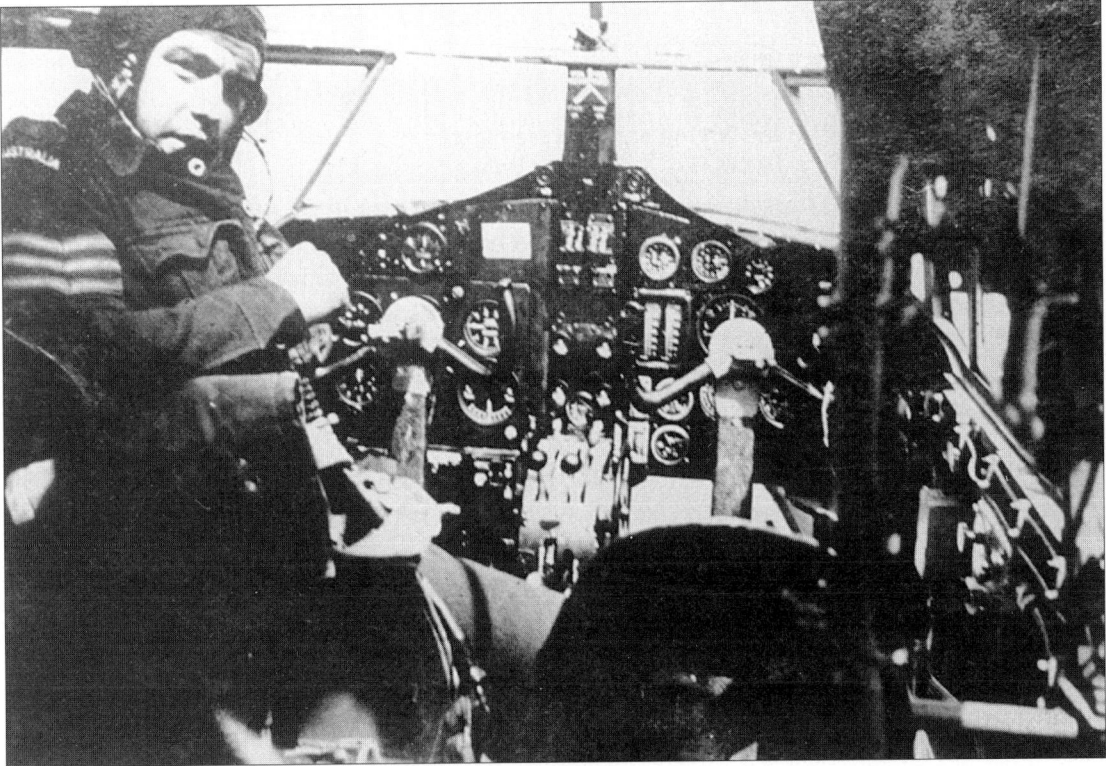

'Bill' Berry at the controls of a Ramsbury based Airspeed Oxford. (E. Berry)

The six to eight week long training programme at Ramsbury was very intensive, and opportunities for pupils to visit the surrounding area were infrequent. Several, including 'Bill' Berry and his friend Noel Davis, managed to visit the village on a number of occasions, and enjoyed a few pints of beer in the local pubs. They found people quiet but friendly, and welcomed the peace away from the noise of the airfield.

On one occasion the pair managed to secure a 48 hour pass and decided to visit Worcester. Unfortunately when the time came for them to return home they found that their train had been cancelled (an all too common occurrence during this period). They phoned their Flight Commander and told him the 'good news'. After the obligatory 'roasting', he calmed down and informed them that a trainee pilot was doing a navigation exercise with a staff pilot in that area, and he would instruct them to land at Worcester and pick up Bill and Noel. At this point he stressed how illegal this procedure was and that they were not to enter any details into their log books.

The Oxford duly arrived and picked up its passengers, the pilot turned into the wind, opened the throttles and raced down the grass strip. The aircraft was barely airborne when the pilot retracted the undercarriage. To the dismay of all on board, the plane sank to the ground, resulting in pieces of propeller and other debris flying in all directions. Fortunately nothing more than pride was hurt. The Flight Commander, pupil pilot and staff pilot were all severely reprimanded for this incident. Ironically, the only ones to escape without a blemish on their records were Flight Sergeants Berry and Davis! Nothing more was heard of this incident and both went on to successfully complete the course.

Listed below are several other local crashes involving Airspeed Oxfords of No.15(P)AFU during 1943:

19/2/43   Oxford I P9034 ran away unmanned on the airfield and hit N3572 (see text).

2/3/43   Oxford I V3335 hit tree on approach at night – pilot killed (see text).

21/3/43   Oxford II AB725 low flying accident (see text).

1/5/43   Oxford I BG272 was hit on runway by V3562 (Oxford I).

11/5/43   Oxford I L4534 crashed on landing (this was the prototype Airspeed Oxford).

27/5/43   Oxford I V3949 collided with ED136 (Oxford II) and crashed near the perimeter. Pilot of V3949 Sgt. P.R.S. Miller (RNZAF) was killed. He had been warned only the previous day to keep a more strict lookout.

7/6/43   Oxford II R6388 dived into ground on cross country flight. Sgt. K.S. Deacon (RAAF) was killed (see text).

25/6/43   Oxford I LX168 and Oxford I V3955 collided in mid-air near Bishopstone, Wiltshire. All occupants were killed.

4/7/43   Oxford II R6097 crashed attempting a forced landing.

20/7/43   Mid-air collision between Oxford I BG236 and Oxford I HN721. Three killed and one seriously injured.

25/8/43   Sgt. L.G. Leatherhead (1316964) killed when Oxford aircraft crashed just after take-off on a solo night flight.

19/9/43   Oxford I HM907 stalled after night take off. Flight Sgt. R. Frith (RAAF) killed.

The inexperience of the young pupil pilots probably accounted for many of these accidents as the Oxford was a very unforgiving aircraft, especially if it was incorrectly trimmed. John Aitken, a New Zealand pupil trained at Ramsbury during 1943 recalls, "If a strong wind was blowing from the south the landing approach would normally take the aircraft over the village, and there was always a downdraught where the hill dropped from the airfield to the river. Sometimes this downdraught was as much as an Oxford could cope with and resulted in pilots losing control."

The first incident listed above (19th February) deserves further explanation. A Royal Australian Air Force pupil had just completed his solo exercises and had taxied his aircraft on to a dispersal point. Unfortunately the area was not on level ground and the pilot had omitted to put on the brakes or wait for the ground crew to place chocks in front of the wheels. As he left the Oxford it moved some distance forward and hit N3572 causing damage to both aircraft. As a result the pilot was sent to Hereford on a three week disciplinary course.

One further accident, not involving a Ramsbury-based aircraft, occurred during the early hours of 4th August 1943. A Wellington III (BJ585), on a cross country flight from 16 OTU at Upper Heyford, began losing oil from its starboard engine. The pilot requested a priority landing, but nearby enemy activity prevented the runway lights from being switched on. Nevertheless the pilot felt compelled to attempt a forced landing. Unfortunately the plane hit a row of elm trees and crashed into a field about a quarter of a mile east of Ambrose Farm where it caught fire. The resulting explosions of ammunition and fuel woke up many village residents, some of whom still remember the incident to this day.

Of the five crew on board BJ585 that night three were killed; the pilot – Sgt. G. Wilson, Bomb Aimer – P/O R.W. Papineau, and Navigator – Sergeant J. Charlier. The other crew members (Wireless Operator – Sergeant L. Phillips, and Rear Gunner – Sergeant S.J. Angus) were seriously injured.

The aircraft

During its existence No.15(P)AFU was mainly equipped with the Airspeed Oxford. This aircraft first entered service during 1937 and quickly became the RAF's principle twin engined trainer. Two variants of the type were produced, and the only external difference between them was the dorsal gun turret, which was fitted solely to the MKI. However the turret was removable, and many MKIs flew in this turretless configuration for much of their service lives. Both types were used extensively by No.15(P)AFU during their stay at Ramsbury, and about 30 Oxfords were normally resident at any one time.

The unit also had several Avro Ansons and one in particular, N5262, seems to have been regularly used at Ramsbury from the beginning of August until the Unit left in October. The Anson was the first modern monoplane ordered in large quantities by the RAF and was a relatively friendly aircraft to fly. Unfortunately it was not considered advanced enough to train aircrew for the new modern bombers then coming into service, and was quickly superseded by the Oxford. N5262 was put to good use for navigational training and as a communications aircraft, regularly ferrying personnel, spares and equipment all over southern England.

Airspeed Oxford MKII R5946 pictured while flying on exercise from Ramsbury.
The pilot at the controls was Noel Davis, an Australian. (E. Berry)

The Instructors

These experienced pilots, some of whom had completed a tour of operations with Bomber Command, taught the pupils flying and navigation. A typical day for a Navigation Instructor would consist of two half-day sessions, one flying, and the other giving classroom lectures. Here the pupils learned about map reading, meteorology, compass errors (variation and deviation) and the odd tricks of altimeters and giro-compasses. When the weather was bad the pupils were shown films on subjects such as the formation of fog or German interrogation methods. Lecturing was unpopular as both instructors and pupils preferred flying.

It was unnecessary for the Flying Instructors to give classroom lectures, a fact that caused some banter with their Navigational colleagues. On the other hand, they generally took greater risks particularly when on low flying exercises.

Free time during the evenings was spent either in the mess or one of the local pubs. During days off (never more than one a week) they sometimes ventured as far as Newbury for a tea-room lunch or a tour of the tobacconists.

Ground Crew

On a normal working day the ground crew would cycle to the mess for breakfast (most personnel were issued with a service bicycle) and then continue the journey around the perimeter track to the flight line. There the aircraft pickets would be untied, engine and cockpit covers removed and the daily routine of inspections completed and signed for. Throughout the day unserviceable aircraft were attended to, aircraft in use were marshalled in and out as required and refuelled as necessary. On flying days one fully crewed fire tender and ambulance would be stationed beside the Control Tower, ready to move at a moment's notice should trouble occur. At the end of the day when flying had ceased the aircraft were picketed down, fuel tanks topped up and the covers fitted.

The weary personnel would then cycle back to their huts for a wash and brush up before heading to the mess or NAAFI. On some evenings if a trip out of camp had been planned, a quick change into 'best blue' would be required. Once again bicycles were utilised by the men for these excursions, sometimes in numbers reminiscent of pre-war cycling club events.

Instructors and ground crew in front of an Oxford on dispersal at Ramsbury.
The lady in the centre drove a van for one of the voluntary organisations.(I. Cooke)

The crew of a Bedford 6 ton Prime Mover and its 1,750 gallon petrol bowser, pose for the photographer on a hot sunny day. The Alsatian dog 'Wolf' was owned by Johnny De La Tasse (second from left). Johnny, who was a fitter on 'W' Flight, had to seek special permission from the base Commander to keep the animal.(I. Cooke)

The WAAFs

The Women's Auxiliary Air Force (WAAF) contingent at Ramsbury was about 60 strong, many of whom were employed as parachute packers, cooks, drivers, storekeepers or administrators.

When they first arrived in December 1942 there was an acute shortage of fuel for the stoves in their barracks, and they found it very difficult to keep warm. Mrs Doris Fielding, who in 1943 was an Administration Sergeant remembers, "wearing every knitted woollen item of clothing that I possessed. Even while on duty in the offices I kept my greatcoat on! On one particular evening I made a fire from a piece of lino and a board which had been used by workmen for mixing up cement. However, by mid-February increased supplies of coke had arrived and things gradually began to improve."

Mrs Fielding also remembers how spread out the camp was and that obtaining a bicycle became an urgent priority. She also recalls how steep the hill always seemed when returning from a night out in the village. During the autumn a friendly farmer who lived near the bottom of the hill would leave baskets of apples beside the road, from which the passing personnel could help themselves on their way back to camp.

Sunday church attendance was compulsory for all WAAF personnel, and services were normally held at Froxfield. Many of the women complained saying that they would prefer it if the services were voluntary. After some debate this was agreed, and then nobody bothered to go!

The normal curfew time for the girls returning to camp after a night out was 22:00 hrs. There were no excuses for being late and a very careful watch was kept whenever they went into the village, after all, there were Americans stationed there! The girls preferred the Americans to the

British lads because of their smart appearance and generosity, and would often return to camp laden with gifts such as chocolates, cigarettes and nylons.

By the end of 1943 WAAFs represented 20% of the RAF's total Home Command strength, and their contribution played a vital part in the victory over Nazi Germany.

WAAF personnel from Ramsbury marching through Hungerford during the town's 'Spitfire week' in 1943. The banner on the bridge reads, "OUR SPITS TO BEAT FRITZ. £50,000 FOR TEN SPITFIRES". (L.B. Jones)

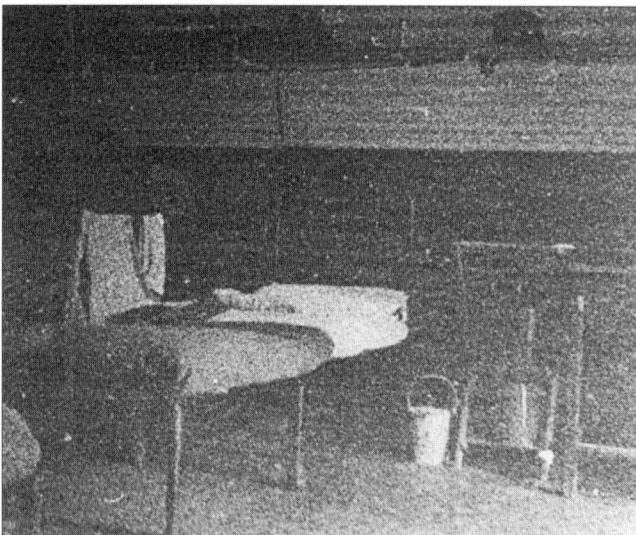

Left and facing page, top left
These pictures were taken by John Aitken, a New Zealand pilot, who underwent some of his flying training at Ramsbury during 1943. John always carried a small half frame folding camera with him and took these snaps of his quarters. He processed and printed them in his Nissen hut without proper blackout or safelight. The results, although of poor quality, are nevertheless an excellent record of the off-duty side of service life during this period. (Both photographs J. Aitken)

The photographer had to be careful when he took this picture of John Aitken, for unofficial photography was an offence which carried severe penalties. (J. Aitken)

Instructors and pupils cutting grass on the aerodrome during the summer of 1943. They are from left to right: P/O Marsh, F/Lt. Baxter (O/C 'K' Flight), Sgt. Couper and Sgt. Croft. Note the ubiquitous bicycles in the background. (T. Parsons)

Moving out

During August and September, rumours spread through the camp that No.15(P)AFU would be moving out to make way for the Ninth USAAF. The unit eventually departed at the end of October; one group moving to Babdown Farm in Gloucestershire and the remainder to Castle Combe in Wiltshire. The Americans took command at the beginning of November and RAF Ramsbury became USAAF Station No. 469.

Although the RAF had departed, a small number of personnel remained to keep the airfield open and they witnessed the arrival of the first group of American servicemen. Mr L. Jones, then an NCO assigned to the care and maintenance party, remembers how pleased most of them were to meet the GIs. "The Americans were very generous and I can remember being given cartons of cigarettes. Getting a lift to Hungerford station was no longer a problem and transport would always be waiting for us when we returned from weekend breaks. Their rations were also much better than ours, but we disliked having all of our meal (main course and dessert) served on one sectioned tray. Because of this they allowed us to have two plates, but we had to wash them up ourselves!" Ivan Cooke remembers being joined by a number of American service technicians who were assembling WACO gliders. "Despite the fact that these Yanks were merely ground personnel, they all wore flying suits and constantly smoked large cigars."

By the beginning of 1944 the Americans were established on the airfield, and the skies over Ramsbury began to fill with the sights and sounds of C-47 transport aircraft, gliders and parachutists, scenes which were to become evermore familiar as the training intensified in preparation for D-Day.

The majority of No.15(P)AFU aircraft were normally dispersed at the western end of the airfield near Park Farm, where this photograph was taken. (E. Berry)

The 437th TCG move in

During November 1943 a USAAF Station Complement Squadron arrived to take over from the RAF, but it was December before the first flying units of the Ninth USAAF arrived. They were the air echelons of the 434th and 435th TCGs who spent their time exercising with the 101st Airborne Division. Both Groups departed to Leicestershire during January 1944, the 434th moving to Fulbeck and the 435th to Langar.

On 5th February the first aircraft from the 437th TCG flew into Ramsbury. The air echelon had left West Palm Beach in the USA at the beginning of January and travelled across the Atlantic via the southern ferry route. The first leg of this arduous journey took them to Puerto Rico, British Guiana (now Guyana), Brazil and Ascension Island, where the group made an over night stop. The following day they continued their flight via Liberia to Marrakech, where they were able to pause and spend some time sampling the sights and sounds of this mysterious North African city. The final leg of their journey to England took the group across the Bay of Biscay to RAF St. Mawgan, near Newquay in Cornwall. On 21st January the group moved on to Balderton, near Nottingham. At Balderton the aircraft had their squadron identification markings applied, whilst the group acclimatised themselves for a week or so, before moving on to Ramsbury.

On 30th January the ground echelon of the 437th left New York aboard the Cunard Liner 'Mauritania', arriving in Liverpool 13 days later. They disembarked and immediately left by train for Hungerford, arriving at two o'clock in the morning. British lorries were waiting at the station to take them and their belongings on the short journey to the airfield.

The 437th TCG was an element of the 53rd Troop Carrier Wing (TCW) of the Ninth USAAF. The entire Wing, which had originally been grouped around Grantham in Lincolnshire, was moved southwards to the Newbury area in order to shorten the glider haul on D-Day, and to be closer to the 101st Airborne Division whose headquarters were at Greenham Lodge, near Newbury.

Each group of the 53rd TCW was equipped with about 72 Douglas C-47 transport aircraft (the military version of the civilian DC-3). This type of aircraft (which the British named 'Dakota') proved to be so successful in the transportation role, that it quickly became the mainstay for the Allies' work in this field.

Troop carrier markings

The 53rd TCW was split into five groups. Each group was sub-divided into four squadrons and each squadron was given a code. A listing of the groups and their squadron codes is given in the table below.

53rd Troop Carrier Wing

Station	Group	Squadrons and their codes			
Aldermaston	434th TCG	71st-CJ	72nd-CU	73rd-CN	74th-ID
Welford	435th TCG	75th-SH	76th-CW	77th-IB	78th-CM
Membury	436th TCG	79th-S6	80th-7D	81st-U5	82nd-3D
Ramsbury	437th TCG	83rd-T2	84th-Z8	85th-9O	86th-5K
Greenham Common	438th TCG	87th-3X	88th-M2	89th-4U	90th-Q7

An aerial photograph showing Ramsbury airfield and village on 9th March 1944. Each of the 437th TCG's four squadrons had 18 C-47 aircraft. There are approximately 50 C-47s and 50 gliders visible here, suggesting that one squadron was 'up' on exercise at the time.
(Reproduced by permission of RCHME)

(Above) C-47 aircraft lined up on the main runway together with Waco CG-4A and Horsa gliders. (US Archives)

(Right) Nine C-47s in a 'V of V' formation fly over Ramsbury airfield, heading south. (G. Theorin)

(Below) Practice parachute jumps, a regular sight in the skies above Ramsbury during the spring and summer of 1944. (J. Reeder)

These codes were painted just aft of the pilot's compartment and were block characters between 36 and 48 inches in height. The aircraft's individual identification letter was positioned on the vertical fin above the serial number.

For D-Day, 24 inch-wide black and white invasion stripes were painted completely around the wings and rear fuselage. The stripes on all upper surfaces were removed two or three weeks later. On the fuselage, to the rear of the cockpit, mission symbols were often applied.

Daily life

The first English meal prepared for men of the 437th TCG was a breakfast of powdered eggs, salty bacon and bitter coffee, and came as a shock to the young Americans who were accustomed to the ample non-rationed meals they had had back home in the United States. Further shocks were to follow!

February of 1944 was a cold and inhospitable month and trying to keep the Nissen huts (sleeping quarters for most of the GIs) warm and comfortable was a difficult task. Normally 12 men were assigned to each hut and their beds were generally arranged six to each side of the room. In the centre of the room was a small cast iron stove. Unfortunately, even when red hot, the heat from the stove seemed to benefit the birds on the roof more than the men inside!

Bathing was another problem. The bath house was made of concrete and most of its window panes had been broken. The water was heated by a boiler in a small shed to the rear of the building; unfortunately there was very little coke available to feed this device and as a consequence all bathing was done in cold water! The Americans partially overcame this problem by stealing coke from the fuel compound, but following persistent protests from the British, this pilfering had to stop. However the Station Commander stepped in and resolved the problem by making extra coke available and bathing could then take place three nights a week.

The airfield personnel looked forward to their free time and the nearby pubs and shops were frequently visited. The village boasted an excellent antique shop owned by Mr Pullen from where many fine pieces of silver and plate were purchased and taken back to the States after the war. The village also had two small bakeries where the traditional Wiltshire lardy cakes could be purchased. Situated in the High Street was a barber's shop run by Mr W.A. Smith and his daughter Rosemary. In 1944 Rosemary was an attractive teenager, and this may have been one reason why so many soldiers visited her father's shop. Rosemary recalls, "My father always got annoyed because they all preferred me to cut their hair and shave them. The arrival of so many Americans into the village increased our business considerably."

Swindon, the nearest large town, was visited each evening by a convoy of GI trucks known as 'The Liberty Run'. They left the group mess hall at 18:00 hrs for the 15 mile journey, returning at 23:00 hrs. Any man missing the return run faced the discomfort of a long walk back. Swindon had several hotels where meals could be bought, there was also a cinema and on Saturday nights public dances were held in the town hall.

London was the GI's favourite destination, where just about any form of entertainment could be found. There were few Americans, having secured a 48 hour pass or seven days leave, who failed to visit the capital city at least once. Some toured its historic buildings, others saw shows at West End theatres, and almost all visited Rainbow Corner, the largest American Red Cross club in Britain, situated in Shaftesbury Avenue. Here the homesick GI could play Juke-Boxes, have his hair cut in a 'home town' barber shop, 'shoot pool' in the games room or visit the library.

The GIs enjoyed life to the full during their brief periods of leave, uncertain, like all men preparing for battle, of what the future might bring. Once back at the airfield the relentless pressure of training continued and helped take their minds off what lay ahead.

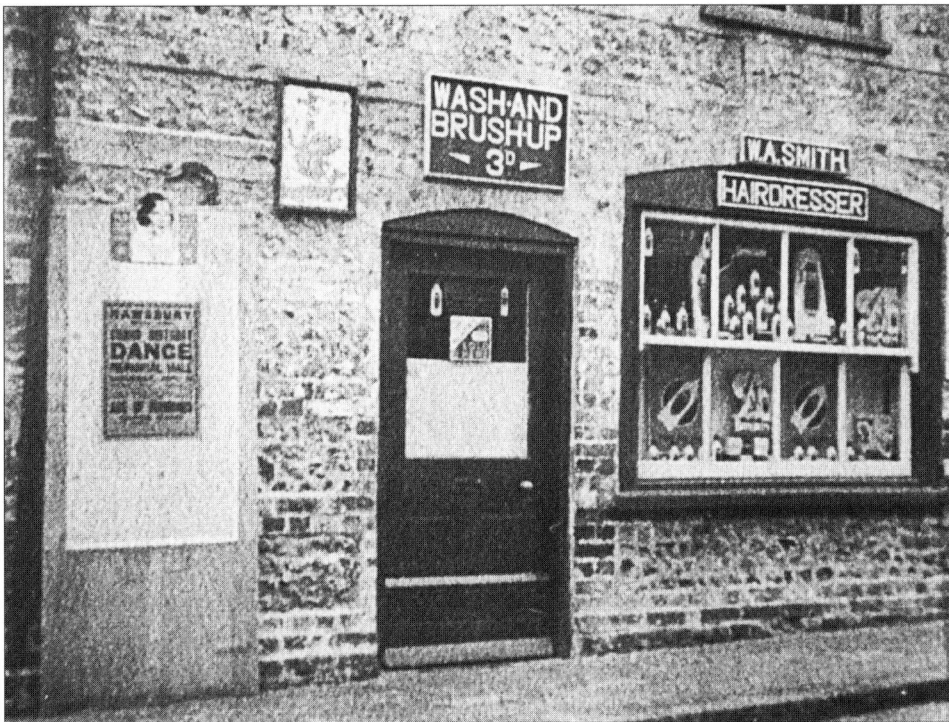

Mr Smith's Barbers shop in the High Street which he ran with help from his daughter Rosemary. The Americans enjoyed the novelty of having their hair cut by a 'lady barber' something unheard-of in the United States. (Mrs R. Connor)

Power and glider pilots from the 85th Squadron standing beside a Nissen hut on a cold winter's day. (G. Theorin)

Life in a Nissen hut

This cartoon was drawn by Charles Waltman, a pilot in the 84th Troop Carrier Squadron, shortly after his arrival at Ramsbury in February 1944. It clearly illustrates the Americans dislike for their new home.

The interior of a Nissen at Ramsbury (now demolished) photographed in 1978. This scene must have been very similar to that which greeted the newly arrived Americans 34 years earlier. (Author)

Training up to D-Day

The 437th TCG started training at the beginning of March and carried on almost continuously in the months leading up to D-Day, subject only to the vagaries of the English weather.

Initially, emphasis was placed on getting the Group's pilots, both glider and powered, proficient in flying and towing the British Horsa glider. The controls and flying characteristics of this aircraft differed considerably from the American CG-4A glider on which all the pilots had been trained in the United States. The CG-4A was the smaller of the two, having an overall length of just over 48 feet. It was constructed of steel tubing covered with a fabric material and could carry 16 fully armed troops or one Jeep. The Airspeed Horsa was very different, being manufactured almost entirely from plywood. The glider was 67 feet long and could carry 29 troops or one Jeep and an artillery piece.

Jim Skidmore, a pilot in the 86th Squadron recalls, "There was a very noticeable difference between the two types when being towed in flight by a C-47. One reason for this, in addition to the obvious difference in size and weight, was the material used in the manufacture of the tow ropes. The Horsa was provided with a hemp rope which seemed to lack any 'give' whatsoever, whereas the CG-4A had a nylon tow rope which possessed a certain amount of elasticity." Jack Whipple, a glider pilot attached to the 83rd Squadron, flew both glider types, taking a Horsa into Normandy on D-Day and flying CG-4As on both of his other combat missions. Jack recalls, "I preferred the CG-4A because I had more experience on the type and it was also a little more forgiving and easier to fly and land. However I did not dislike the Horsa, and considered it to be a very fine aircraft which flew very well."

Training consisted of formation flying, glider towing and instrument flying. Also the Group practised actual and simulated paratroop missions, and much emphasis was placed upon pre-dawn take-off and marshalling of aircraft. This was necessary because the initial assault stages of the forthcoming invasion were planned to take place under the cover of darkness.

At the end of formation flight practice, the aircraft and glider combinations would return to Ramsbury where the glider would be released to come swooping down out of the dawn sky and land on the grass infield of the base. After the gliders had landed the C-47s would return and fly one by one past the Control Tower, dropping their tow ropes on to the ground. Later the ropes were retrieved by the glider mechanics for re-use. The planes would then land and the crews would be debriefed, before going to bed.

The high concentration of aircraft in this area meant that incidents during training were inevitable. On 4th March 1944 the 437th TCG suffered one of its worst flying accidents. The Group had taken off during the early evening on a simulated paratroop drop. The weather at take-off was cold and clear, but after they had been up for about 45 minutes they ran into heavy cloud and returned to base.

A few aircraft managed to land at Ramsbury before a snowstorm closed the field. The rest had to find alternative places to land, some proceeded to Membury and others to Welford. Unfortunately one aircraft (serial No. 2100586) from the 84th Squadron had completely lost its way in the atrocious conditions. There were three crew members on board; the pilot 1st Lt. Lloyd Sloan, co-pilot 2nd Lt. Richard Clark and radio operator Sgt. Harold Pope. In addition the plane was carrying two paratroopers. It seems that they may have been trying to land the aircraft in an open field near Chisbury, but while making their approach hit a Beech tree beside a pond, about 200 yards east of Horsehall Hill Farm. The aircraft then crashed into Heron's Point Wood and caught fire.

Living at Horsehall Hill Farm at the time was 11 year old David Kady. He links the time of the crash quite clearly with his father's habit of 'popping out for a pint' between 9 and 10 o'clock in the evening. David's mother, after hearing the noise, went around to her neighbour and asked him to go and see what had happened but he refused. About half an hour later Stanley Kady returned home and made his way to the crash site. He was the first person on the scene but, despite managing to pull one of the pilots clear of the burning plane, he was unable to save the lives of the crew.

Only seven days later, the 437th TCG suffered a further setback. During a routine glider tow training mission, a Horsa glider (LG891) became detached from its tow plane and landed in a small ploughed field near the village school in Axford.

The pilot of the C-47 tow plane (42100877), Major Donald Bradley, inspected the field and decided that it would be possible to pull the glider out. He flew back to Ramsbury for a new towrope, and with Lt. Gaylord Strong flying as co pilot and Captain Lee Gillette (the 83rd Squadron Flight Surgeon) as an observer, they returned to the field. Major Bradley landed without difficulty and attached the new towrope. Meanwhile 'Doc' Gillette stationed an ambulance at the far end of the field.

All three then climbed aboard the C-47 aircraft, Major Bradley sitting in the left-hand cockpit seat, Lt. Strong on his right and 'Doc' Gillette below the Astro Dome. The brakes were released, and the plane slowly picked up speed. As it became airborne it struck some power cables which ran along the southern boundary of the field causing it to pitch into the ground, eventually coming to a rest in the River Kennet. The glider pilot, although unable to see the tow aircraft through a cloud of dust, saw the flash of sparks as the C-47 hit the power cables. He cut loose and glided across the valley to another field for a safe landing.

Major Bradley suffered serious head injuries and died one hour later. Lt. Strong was also seriously injured and died two days later in Burdrop hospital. 'Doc' Gillette suffered severe damage to his back and was hospitalised for over a month, but eventually returned to his duties and remained with the group until the end of the war.

Wreckage of C-47 aircraft (42100877) which crashed at Axford in March 1944. (L. Gillette via N. Stevens)

Flying Circus

On 24th May 1944 Ramsbury was visited by an unusual assortment of British, American and German aircraft. This 'flying circus' was formed at Thorney Island earlier in the month, and visited allied bases and airfields in the weeks leading up to D-Day to give troops a close-up view of the types of aircraft that would soon become familiar sights.

Included in this 'circus' were aircraft from 1426 (Enemy Aircraft) Flight RAF. This unit had been formed at Duxford in November 1941 and was often referred to by the Press as the 'Rafwaffe'. On 12th March 1943 the flight moved to Collyweston, near Wittering, and this was to remain its home until it was disbanded on 31st January 1945. The Flight consisted entirely of captured enemy aircraft, which following evaluation by the Royal Aircraft Establishment (RAE) at Farnborough, were handed over to the flight who toured the country giving static and flying demonstrations, mostly to fighter and bomber units.

Focke Wulf 190 A-4 (RAF serial No. PN999) at Ramsbury on 24th May 1944. This particular fighter was captured on 20th June 1943 after it had landed in error at RAF Manston in Kent. After tests by the RAE at Farnborough and the Aircraft and Armament Experimental Establishment (A & AEE) at Boscombe Down, it was handed over to 1426 (Enemy Aircraft) Flight on 28th September. Other aircraft visible in this picture are from left to right, Martin B-26 Marauder, Mitchell, Hawker Hurricane and Douglas C-47. In the distance there can be seen some of the numerous Airspeed Horsa and Waco CG-4A gliders. These gliders were just two short weeks away from their baptism of fire.
(J. Antrim via N. Stevens)

(Above) Taxiing past one of Ramsbury's T2 type hangers is a Martin B-26 Marauder of the 553rd Bomb Squadron, 386th Bomb Group, Ninth USAAF. (J. Antrim via N. Stevens)

Facing page

(Top) On 21st July 1940 this Messerschmitt Bf 110 took off from its base in the Cherbourg area on a photo reconnaissance mission. Intercepted by Hurricanes of No. 238 Squadron from RAF Westhampnett (Goodwood), near Chichester, it force-landed at Goodwood House Farm. Repairs were carried out using parts from another Bf 110 C-5 shot down near Wareham, Dorset. The aircraft was allocated the RAF serial No. AX772 and after extensive evaluation at RAE Farnborough it finally arrived at No. 1426 (Enemy Aircraft) Flight on 5th March 1942. AX772 is seen here during its visit to Ramsbury on 24th May 1944. (M. Demuth)

(Bottom) In the immediate foreground stands a Mustang and behind it a P-47 Thunderbolt belonging to the 551st Fighter Squadron, 495th Fighter Training Group, Eighth USAAF. In the background from left to right can be seen an Albemarle, several Airspeed Horsa gliders, Douglas C-47, Waco CG-4A glider, Martin B-26 Marauder and a Mosquito. (J. Antrim via N. Stevens)

D-Day – 6th June 1944

Sitting in the garden of 'Elm Bank' at Whittonditch on the evening of 5th June 1944, John Day was enjoying the last rays of sunshine of that early summer's day. He heard the drone of aircraft engines and gazed skyward to see massed formations of Allied bombers heading south. There was nothing particularly unusual about this as many bombers had passed this way during the previous weeks. However on this particular evening there were more aircraft and formations than he could ever remember seeing before, and he wondered what was going on. In the days that followed, as the success of the Allied landings in France became evident, John realised that he had witnessed the opening phase of the largest combined air and seaborne invasion in history.

The operation was code-named 'Overlord' and its initial assault phase was entitled 'Neptune'. This called for six massed glider landings, four from the 82nd Airborne Division coded 'Detroit', 'Elmira', 'Galveston' and 'Hackensack', and two from the 101st Airborne Division coded 'Chicago' and 'Keokuk'.

The 437th TCG took part in operations 'Detroit' and 'Elmira' which set off at 01:59 and 19:07 hrs respectively on D-Day, and Operation 'Galveston' which departed at 04:39 hrs on D-Day plus 1 (7th June). All gliders were single towed and the weather over the Channel on D-Day was good, with visibility about ten miles; however a cloud bank covered the approach to the French coast.

A week or so earlier, on 29th May, 18 aircraft and crews of the 85th Squadron temporarily joined squadrons of the 436th TCG at nearby Membury. From there they took part in the mission code-named 'Albany,' transporting paratroopers of the 101st Airborne Division to Normandy before returning to Membury. Later that same morning they re-joined their parent group at Ramsbury.

Facing page

*(**Top**) This picture, taken a few days prior to D-Day, shows Airspeed Horsa and Waco CG-4A gliders drawn up on Ramsbury airfield. Some are still waiting to have their distinctive black and white invasion stripes applied, and it's interesting to note that the Horsa gliders on the right of the picture still retain their original RAF roundels. (Imperial War Museum)*

*(**Bottom**) An 85th TCS C-47 returns to its home base following the squadrons detached service with the 436th TCG at Membury, where it flew one combat mission on D-Day. In the centre of the picture, below the aircraft, Ramsbury's three main runways are clearly visible. (M. Demuth via N. Stevens)*

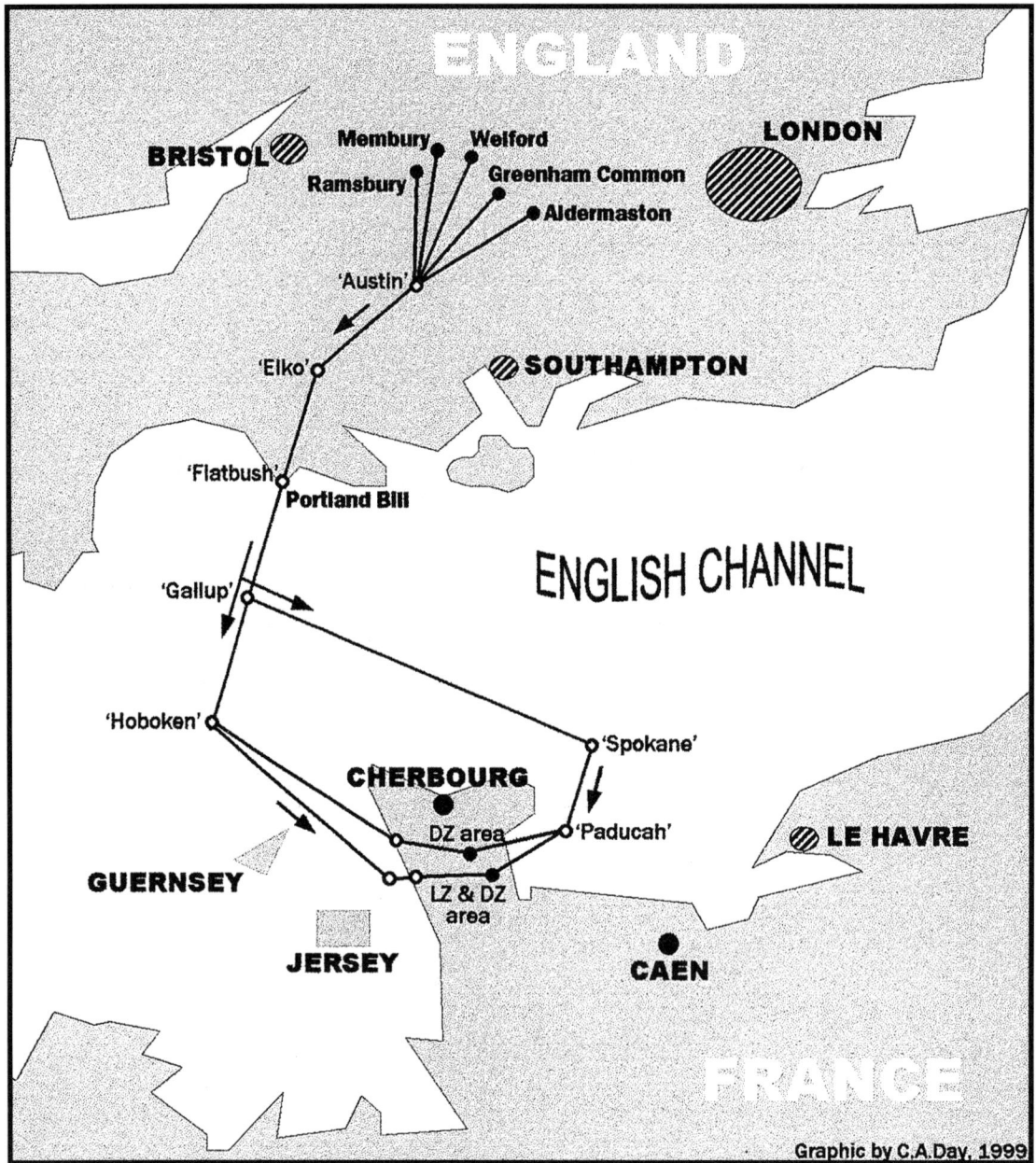

Map showing the planned flight path of the 53rd TCW on D-Day.

Take-off

As May gave way to June, the high pressure over the British Isles moved away and was replaced by a deepening depression. On 23rd May Gen. Eisenhower had established the date for the invasion as June 5th, but as the planners anxiously watched the weather charts it became clear that a postponement of 24 hours would be necessary.

The soldiers of the 82nd Airborne Division, waiting by their aircraft at Ramsbury during the evening of 5th June, would be amongst the first going into action on D-Day. Most wore winter clothing against the cold damp wind that blew across the open expanse of the airfield.

In the village, most inhabitants were asleep. The noise of aircraft moving into position and preparing to take-off disturbed a few of them, but there was nothing unusual about this as there had been many other noisy exercises over the preceding months.

On the airfield the crews received their final briefing. As the men listened, their thoughts drifted back to the many instructions they had received over the previous days. Jack Merrick, from the 84th Squadron, who piloted the 51st and penultimate glider in the initial formation, remembers, "We had been shown detailed maps of Normandy and briefed fully about our part in the operation. From that moment onwards we were prevented from talking to anybody who was not taking part in the mission, and we moved about the camp in groups, escorted by armed guards". With the final briefing over, the group chaplain Captain Jesse Woods, read from the 91st Psalm. Jack remembers, "I tried to listen to what he had to say but I was not overly religious at that time and my mind was concentrating on the flight ahead." Colonel Cedric Hudgens then read the order of the day from Gen. Eisenhower. At last the crews climbed aboard their aircraft and nervously readied themselves for the trip across the Channel to France.

Serial 28 of Operation 'Detroit' was the first to leave. Its destination was the fields north of St. Mere-Eglise, and the arrival time was set for 04:00 hrs.

The first of the 52 plane and glider combinations to leave the runway at Ramsbury on that historic day was:

Aircraft C-47
Serial number 42-10870 'Feeble Eagle'.
Pilot: Col. Cedric E. Hudgens (Flight Commander and left column leader)
Co-pilot: 1st Lt. Thomas F. Rataiczak
Navigator: 2nd Lt. Edmund G. Wydick
Crew Chief: T. Sgt. Weber L. Ackman
Radio Operator: Sgt. Harold L. Atkins

Glider CG-4A
Serial number 42-46521
Pilot: Captain Willis T. Evans
Co-pilot: F.O. Ralph E. Toms
Glider Leader: Maj Faith
Type of Load: Personnel of Div. HQ 82nd Airborne Division.

The green flare arcing into the dark morning sky signalled the lead aircraft to begin its take-off run, and within 30 minutes all 52 combinations had departed. As the heavily-laden craft circled to gain height and form up, one Horsa glider became detached from its tow plane. Despite the darkness and danger of collision with other aircraft the glider was able to make a safe landing near the main runway. A spare C-47 parked in-readiness for such an eventuality moved into position. Meanwhile a weapons carrier quickly brought the glider back to the end of runway 26 where it was attached to the tow aircraft. Remarkably, the pair arrived over the landing zone only thirty minutes behind schedule!

At 05:22, only three hours after the last aircraft of Serial 28 had left England en-route for Normandy, the first C-47 returned. Later that day 26 C-47s towing 18 Horsa and eight Waco CG-4A gliders took off with supplies and reinforcements as part of Operation 'Elmira.' This daylight mission allowed the crews to see at first hand the immensity of Operation 'Overlord' as they flew over the English Channel. Below them were thousands of ships pouring forth a seemingly endless stream of men and machines onto the French shore. For those who saw it, it was a moving and unforgettable sight.

D-Day Plus One

Fifty C-47s of the 437th took off on mission 'Galveston' towing 32 Wacos and 18 Horsas. The following is an extract from the book entitled *The Glider War** and powerfully illustrates the problems which could occur:

> 'Take off began at 04:39 more than half an hour before dawn in poor visibility, rain and gusty winds. A plane towing one Horsa from the 437th with a thousand pound overload could not get the glider moving fast enough for the combination to get off the ground and had to release the glider. The pilot brought it to a stop on the end of the strip. Another was accidentally released en-route and landed near Portland Bill.
>
> One glider combination after another roared down the field. Now it was Lieutenant Rendlemen's turn. The rope of his glider tightened, as it did so the glider nose pulled downward. Rendleman pulled back on the controls and a fraction of a second later the glider was on its way down the runway. Sergeant Edward H. Shimko and his mortar squad sat tensely in the fuselage behind, with twenty-two boxes of anti-tank rifle grenades, an 81mm mortar and thirty-six rounds of mortar ammunition lashed tightly to the floor.
>
> No more than seventy-five feet into take off, when tension of the tow system was greatest, all heard an explosion behind Lieutenant Rendleman. Momentarily no one knew what had happened. Rendleman took little notice his eyes glued ahead in those critical seconds of take off. In a few moments, as he went faster, wind started to blow in behind him. He turned round and saw the runway speeding by underneath. He was now airborne. The glider nose opened at the base looking like a tremendous whale taking a gulp of air, wind shrieked into the opening. Sergeant Shimko threw off his seat belt and jumped to the opening. He grabbed the steel frame work of the nose and struggled to pull it closed. By now several of his men had joined the effort and Rendleman cut loose. The glidermen managed to get some rope around the nose tubing and through some of the lashing rings on the floor of the glider and pulled at the nose until it closed and tied it. Rendleman landed the glider at Ramsbury. There he found an empty glider. Shimko transferred the load and got ready to go. Now Rendleman was at a loss because he was not certain where to land. Colonel Donald French, the Deputy Group Commander, told Rendleman he would tow the glider with a spare plane that was available. Soon they were on their way again.'

* The Glider War by James E. Mrazek. Reproduced by kind permission of the publishers, Robert Hale Limited.

By 08:30 hrs on 7th June the 437th's scheduled D-Day missions had been completed. The Group had suffered losses but fortunately they were minimal and considerably less than had been anticipated.

June to September 1944

The invasion of Normandy had been a remarkable success and as the weeks passed the German army began to fall back. To maintain momentum the Allied troops at the front needed to be regularly re-supplied. Most material arrived via the artificial harbours code-named 'Mulbury' which had been towed across the Channel and assembled at St. Laurent and Arromanches on the Normandy coast. As the advance progressed, further supplies were brought in by air, using newly-constructed advanced landing grounds. The 437th were called upon to deliver petrol, rations, clothing, blood plasma and of course ammunition, much of which came from the vast ammunition dump located in and around Savernake Forest.

Unloading of the planes in France was performed as quickly as possible and in most cases wounded were loaded aboard the aircraft for the return to England. In these instances the planes were always accompanied by American nurses.

Back at Ramsbury the aircraft would be met by medical personnel of the 814th Air Evacuation Squadron, which was stationed on the field. The wounded would then be placed in waiting ambulances and rushed to the nearby American army hospitals.

Shortly after D-Day attempts were made to salvage, for re-use, the gliders which had landed undamaged in Normandy. It was intended that these gliders should be snatched out of the fields by a low-flying C-47 fitted with a trailing hook, which would catch a rope suspended between two poles, and pull the glider in to the air. Eleven men from the 437th went to France to co-ordinate this operation but most of the gliders were too badly damaged, and only 13 were successfully retrieved.

On 12th July the 437th were told they were leaving for Italy to take part in another combat mission. However four aircraft and crews from each squadron remained at Ramsbury to continue with the re-supply work.

This new operation, code-named 'Dragoon', was the invasion of southern France. The aircraft left on 16th July and made for Montalto airfield, about 50 miles north west of Rome. All aircraft had been fitted with cabin fuel tanks as the journey involved a long over water flight, punctuated with a short stopover at Marrakech in Morocco.

Operation 'Dragoon' took place on 15th August. An area around Le Muy in southern France was chosen for the intended drop and landing zones. The invasion was a complete success and after a re-supply drop on the following day the 437th's involvement in this operation was over. For a week or so the detachment remained in Italy on standby before moving on to Gibraltar, where they loaded their aircraft with tax-free whisky and gin. Finally, on the 24th August, they returned to England .

Meanwhile back at Ramsbury the Group's remaining aircraft had been joined by the following units: 98th TCS of the 440th TCG from Exeter, the 301st TCS of the 441st TCG from Merryfield, the 93rd TCS of the 439th TCG from Upottery, and the 306th TCS of the 442nd TCG based at Weston Zoyland. These redeployments allowed an uninterrupted supply of ammunition and fuel to France, despite the 437th's assignment in Italy.

Such was the success of Allied airborne operations, that Chiefs of Staff began to consider new tasks for the airborne soldiers. On 26th August the IX Troop Carrier Command was transferred from the Ninth USAAF to the newly-conceived First Allied Airborne Army. However, as far as the groups and squadrons were concerned, the change meant very little.

At the beginning of September a new plan was conceived. The idea, put forward by General Montgomery, was to seize a road that led from the Belgian border through Holland to the German frontier, capture the bridges along that route and thereby create a corridor directly into the industrial heartland of Germany. It was confidently predicted that success would bring the war to an end before Christmas. This daring operation was code named 'Market Garden' and was set for Sunday, 17th September.

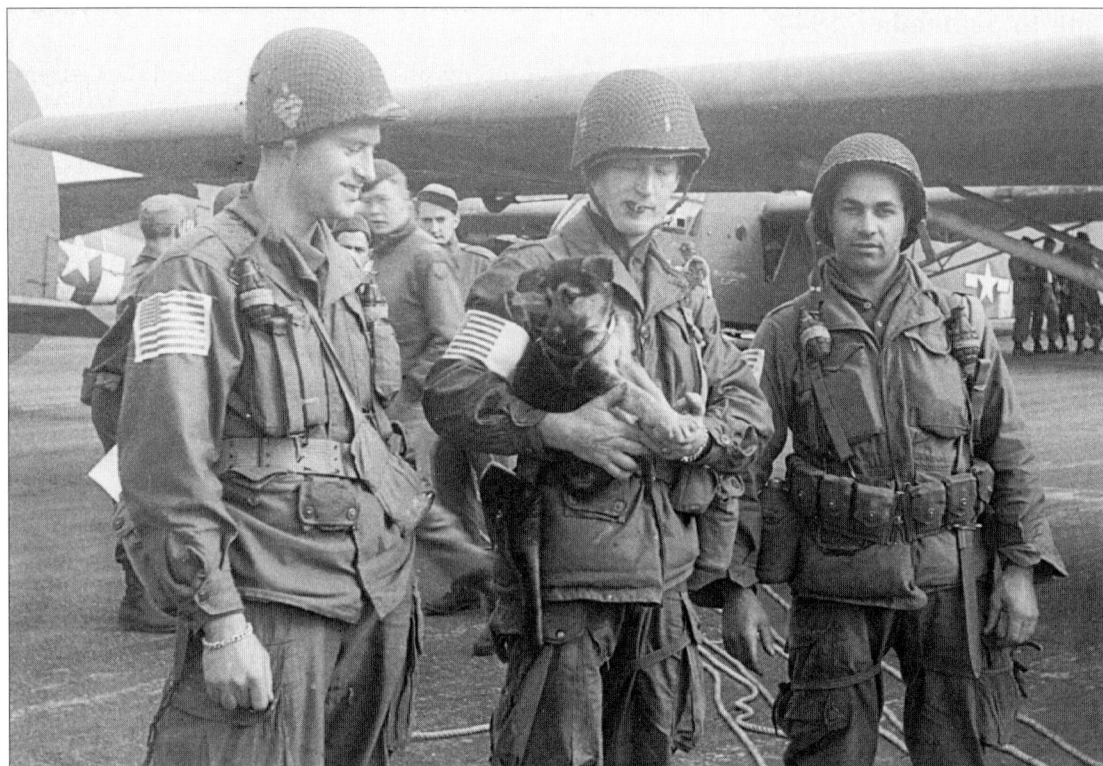

Men of the 101st Airborne Division's 502nd Regiment pose with a canine friend at Ramsbury prior to their departure for Holland on 17th September 1944. (J. Antrim via N. Stevens)

Operation 'Market Garden'

On 12th September units of the 101st Airborne Division moved on to the airfield in preparation for their role in 'Market Garden'. The aircraft and gliders were checked and overhauled, and on the 15th the 437th TCG was briefed. They learned that the mission would take place during daylight hours and that gliders would be flown without co-pilots due to a shortage of trained glider pilots.

The weather on the morning of the 17th was beautiful, and the warm sun shone down on the troops waiting to board their gliders. In Ramsbury church, as in others across the country, a special service was being held to commemorate the RAF's victory over the Luftwaffe during the Battle of Britain. The congregation could hear the noise of the aircraft preparing to leave and knew that another mission was underway. Many of them felt that this was an opportune time and place to pray for the soldiers' safe return.

Seventy aircraft and glider combinations left Ramsbury at 11:00 hrs that morning and joined the mightiest airborne force in history, destination Holland. As this huge airborne armada crossed the eastern counties of England people in their thousands stared up in awe, to witness a spectacle the like of which nobody had ever seen before, nor is ever likely to see again.

This day was to be the darkest in the history of the 437th. The group lost more aircraft on this mission than all their other combat operations put together. A total of eight planes failed to return.

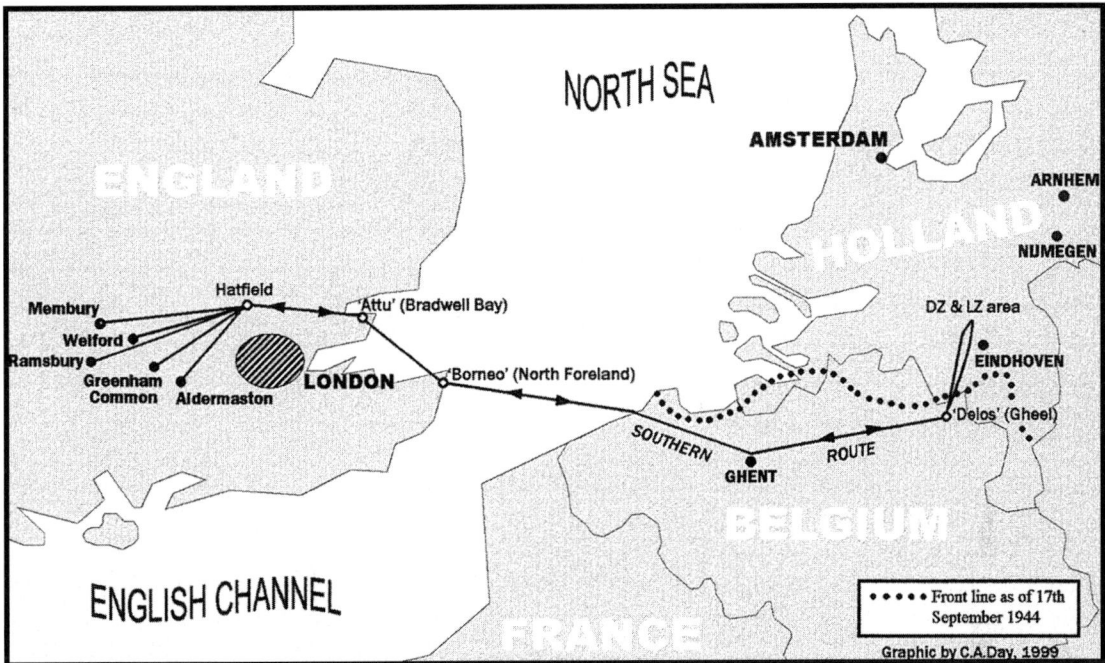

Operation 'Market Garden', 53rd TCW air routes.

Despite this the Group had to prepare for its next mission scheduled for the following day. The routes differed from the previous mission and this time no aircraft were lost, although several were damaged by small-arms fire.

On 19th September the 437th were scheduled to fly a re-supply mission to the paratroopers trapped behind enemy lines. However, due to the losses and damage suffered over the previous two days by the Group, it was impossible to put up a full complement of aircraft. After a discussion with Wing HQ at Greenham Common spare aircraft were ferried in from the 440th TCG at Exeter. These aircraft were brought in by 440th crews, but would be flown into action by men of the 437th. As the first C-47 sped down the runway at 15:00 hrs, the last of the 440th's aircraft were still being loaded with their supplies. Fortunately this mission was uneventful and all planes returned safely.

This was the end of the 437th's involvement in 'Market Garden'. However, on 20th September 12 aircraft of the 442nd TCG which had arrived from Chilbolton flew one mission from Ramsbury, carrying 75mm Howitzers and men of the 377th Parachute Field Artillery.

*(**Above and below**) Ramsbury's crowded main runway looking west on the morning of Sunday, 17th September 1944. Note in the lower photograph how the glider/aircraft communication wire entwines the nylon towrope. (Both photographs J. Antrim via N. Stevens)*

Bastogne

With the 'Market Garden' episode behind them the 437th returned to re-supply and evacuation work. Towards the end of the year, a number of aircraft technicians from each of the Group's four squadrons were assigned to B-24 'Liberator' bomber bases, to learn how to maintain this type of aircraft.

These assignments arose because several B-24 aircraft, modified to carry 5,000 gallons of fuel and re-designated C-109, had been received by the group. The intention was that these would be used to transport fuel to the Continent. The C-109s were highly unpopular and regarded by their crews as potential death traps – for as flying petrol tankers they were highly vulnerable, even to small-arms fire. In addition there were no reinforced runways at forward airstrips on the Continent capable of supporting the weight of these aircraft when fully loaded, and hence the C-109s were never used to their full potential.

With the winter months approaching the weather was becoming the Group's biggest problem. A flight that may have left its base in bright sunshine might then find itself 'socked in' by fog or low cloud and unable to return from the Continent for several days. Consequently all crew members took with them a sleeping bag and essential rations.

For a week or so in mid December a thick fog blanketed southern England. During this period another disaster struck. A C-47 from the Air Transport Command was looking for an accessible airfield, but the plane was running out of fuel. The pilot radioed Ramsbury Control Tower asking permission to land. The runway lights were switched on and flares fired. After several aborted attempts the aircraft made its final approach from the east towards runway 26. At this point misfortune took a hand, for the pilot had misjudged his height and hit the tops of some trees in Whitehill Coppice, a quarter of a mile short of the runway. The impact was only a hundred yards or so away from the 84th Squadron Enlisted Mens' quarters. Crew Chief Ted Pilgram was standing outside his Nissen hut in this area and heard the aircraft crash, "The plane came in very low, only about 20 feet above our hut and hit some trees close by. The trees tore both main wings off, and the fuselage continued on for some distance before coming to a rest. Fortunately the aircraft didn't catch fire and amazingly some of the crew survived." The survivors were taken down into the village and were treated by Doctor Mills at his surgery in Kennet House before being sent on to Burdrop Hospital.

On 16th December, with the weather unchanged, the Germans made what turned out to be their last major attack of the war. They struck at the weakest point on the front line, in the Ardennes forest, and pushed ahead at amazing speed creating a huge bulge in the Allied front line, from which the battle took its name. The small Belgian town of Bastogne commanded a series of road junctions, and Allied Supreme HQ decided that it should be held at all costs. On 18th December the 101st Airborne Division were sent in to defend this area.

The 437th was tasked to drop supplies to the 101st, who were now encircled by the enemy. The fog persisted however, and it was not until 23rd December that they were able to fly their first mission, losing one 85th TCS aircraft to German gunfire.

The weather the following day, Christmas Eve, also proved satisfactory and once again the 437th departed for Belgium. During this period word had been received from High Command, suggesting that German prisoners on the Continent, and in England, might be planning a mass escape to take place on the night of the 24th. As the POW camp at Lambourn Woodlands was only three miles away the rumours were taken very seriously, and all personnel were issued with side arms and live ammunition.

During the night of Christmas Eve Don Bolce, from the 85th Squadron, and some friends decided to play a few tricks on other members of the Group. Don recalls, "We took a big rock and ran down the side of a Nissen hut scraping the stone against the metal roof cladding, which sounded to those inside as if the place was under attack!"

In another hut, one occupant had frequently told his colleagues of a dream he'd had, of a German armed with a flame thrower bursting into their hut and burning them all to a crisp. A few men who shared the hut with him had got very fed up with the story, and decided to teach him a lesson. Whilst the man was asleep they poured some lighter fluid around his bed, set light to it, and then ran outside hitting the roof of the hut and making as much noise as possible. The story of the German and the flame thrower was never heard again!

On Christmas Day flying operations were cancelled as thick fog had descended. However by 10:00 hrs on 26th December the 437th planes were once again racing down the main runway to begin their last re-supply mission to Bastogne.

During the month of January word spread that the Group would soon be moving to France. On 25th February rumour became fact as the 437th left Ramsbury, its home for just over a year, and moved to an airfield known to the Americans simply as A 58, situated near the town of Coulemmiers, some 20 miles east of Paris.

Despite the fact that all American aircraft had now left, the US Ninth Troop Carrier Command still retained control of the base, with rear echelons remaining until June 1945.

A C-109 tanker seen at Ramsbury during January 1945. (B. Quick via N. Stevens)

The Final Years

The return of the Boys in Blue

On 5th June 1945, a month after the war in Europe had ended, USAAF Station No. 469 returned once more to RAF control. It was initially taken over by No. 70 Group Fighter Command, and was again a satellite of Andover. No. 70 Group's tenure was short-lived as on 8th June the Station was transferred to No. 4 Group Transport Command. Still on strength at this time were nine Americans (two officers and seven other ranks) who were responsible for feeding all station personnel. However, by 28th June the last American had left.

At the beginning of July the station became a satellite of Welford, and towards the end of the month F/O George took command from S/L Neate. On 5th September, four Dakotas from Welford practised 'Circuits and Bumps', and this exercise was repeated by a further 19 Dakotas on each of the following two days.

The 15th September saw a further change of command with the arrival of W/C Meharg AFC, who was promptly provided with a Hillman utility van (RAF 66737) as his personal transport. On the same day personnel from 'F' Squadron N.1 Wing, Glider Pilot Regiment, also arrived and were accommodated at one of the recently re-opened dispersed sites.

Dakotas from Welford ferried gliders to Ramsbury, and on 21st September eight Horsa IIs arrived from Cosford, followed soon after by a further seven from Brize Norton. During the middle of October the first glider night flying commenced at the station.

It was on 19th October, during one of these night exercises, that F/Sgt Gooch piloting Horsa Glider TL937 became disorientated. On making his approach he momentarily lost sight of the flare path. He then saw the street lights in Whittonditch Road and, mistakenly thinking that he was back on course, made his descent. Gooch soon realised his error and luckily still had enough height to be able to glide over a row of houses, before landing in a field behind them. The glider eventually stopped on Mr Charles Whiting's allotment, severely damaging his chicken shed and the glider. Fortunately the crew were unhurt. The glider remained in place for about a week, giving the children of the village an exciting new toy.

On 29th October five Dakotas and five Waco Hadrian gliders of the Glider Pick Up Unit (GPU) arrived from Ibsley. The GPU's role was to snatch gliders from the ground without the tow aircraft landing. As mentioned earlier, this technique had been perfected by the Americans. The following day, Horsa TL 301 piloted by F/O Clark (163508) became detached from its aircraft shortly after take-off. The pilot made a 180 degree turn to get back to the aerodrome, but landed in a field a few hundred yards short of the perimeter track, colliding with a building. F/O Clark was detained for a while at Wroughton Hospital.

The 1st November saw the GPU's first full day of training, and three Dakotas made 12 glider snatches. However, the war with Japan was now over and rapid progress had been made in the field of helicopter development; consequently the writing was very much on the wall so far as military gliders were concerned. With this in mind, the GPU was disbanded on 15th November. At the beginning of 1946 the airfield became a satellite of Upavon, when Airspeed Oxfords from 'F' Flight of No. 7 Flying Instructors School arrived under the command of F/Lt Green.

On 24th February S/L Couzens AFC became the very last Commanding Officer at RAF Ramsbury, and at the end of March all flying ceased. However the last recorded military aircraft to use the airfield was a Mk. 22 Spitfire (PK 633) which force landed there on 4th January 1947. By now the status of the base had been downgraded to 'care and maintenance', and it was destined never to be used again as a military airfield.

A Hostel for the Land Girls

During 1947 the military authorities relinquished control of the airfield domestic sites. The Women's Land Army, still a very busy and important source of farm labour, then took control of a small number of these buildings for use as a hostel.

Two dozen or so Land Girls moved on to the site which came under the control of the Wiltshire Agricultural Committee, represented by two local farmers, Messrs Horton and Gauntlet. In charge of the hostel was a Mr Curry.

The girls were directed to any farm where labour was required and were transported there in the camp lorry. This vehicle was usually driven by the diminutive Miss Hillier, who was so small that blocks had to be fitted to the lorries' control pedals so that she could reach them!

Martin Cound was the camp foreman and of particular interest to him was the calf rearing centre, which had been set up on site employing six of the Land Girls.

In a group of buildings not far from the hostel the authorities established another camp for displaced persons. Western Europe was awash with these people, many of whom came from Eastern European countries, having been forced to flee from their homes; firstly by the Germans and then by the Russians. Many of those at Ramsbury were of Polish or Ukrainian descent, and a few of them worked regularly with the Land Girls at the calf rearing centre. Gradually, over the following three years, more permanent homes were found for the newcomers, and the need for camp accommodation fell away.

When, in 1950 the Women's Land Army was finally wound up, the Ramsbury hostel was abandoned and the buildings quickly fell into a state of dereliction.

War Department Auctions

During 1948 several auctions of redundant War Department equipment were held in the hangar at Bridge Farm. At around the same time similar auctions were taking place all across the United Kingdom, where virtually anything could be obtained, from paper clips to tanks! Items offered for sale at Ramsbury included generators, aircraft instruments, filing cabinets and desks.

Gradually the airfield was returned to local farmers, and as time passed nature began to obscure this once important, but short lived feature of the local landscape. In 1954 the hangars were dismantled and by the early 1970s most of the remaining buildings had been demolished. Today the site is again peaceful and quiet, a far cry from those hectic months during the Summer of 1944.

(Above left) Martin Cound and four 'Land Girls' from the hostel. *(Above right)* Milking time.
(Below left) The car in the centre of this picture belonged to Mr Harry Horton from the Wiltshire 'War Ag'.
(Below right) Mr Lemondoski, one of the many displaced people who were temporarily accomodated
at Ramsbury airfield. (All photographs Mrs F. Cound)

(Above and right) The hangar at Bridge Farm being dismantled during 1954. (W.C. Watts)

This group of Nissen huts, photographed at Ramsbury during 1978, were used during the war as officers' sleeping quarters. Unfortunately all of these buildings have now been demolished. (Author)

Dedicated to honor the members of the
437th Troop Carrier Group
United States Army Ninth Air Force
World War II
who were stationed at Ramsbury Airfield
and participated in the campaigns of
Normandy, Ardennes, Northern France,
Rome-Arno, Southern France,
Rhineland and Central Europe.

Where the River Kennet flows over
the small weir below this spot,
Major Donald E. Bradley
and 1st Lt Gaylord Strong
members of the 83rd Squadron,
437th Troop Carrier Group,
died in the crash of a
Douglas Dakota C47 aircraft on
March 11th 1944.
They were attempting to retrieve a
Horsa glider that had broken free
in a practice mission and landed in the
field above this spot.

Captain Lee Gillette, 83rd Squadron
Flight Surgeon, although seriously injured,
survived the accident
after 5 weeks in the
Burderop Park,

CHAPTER 5

RAMSBURY TODAY

American veterans from the 437th TCG held their annual reunion in the Ramsbury area during November 1997, and are seen posing on what remains of runway 26. (C.A. Day)

Victory at last

On Monday, 7th May 1945 at the technical college in the city of Rheims, northern France, General Jold of the German Army signed the surrender document which officially brought the war in Europe to a close. Four months later, on 15th August, a radio broadcast by Emperor Hirohito told the Japanese nation of his decision to surrender. After six long years the war was finally at an end.

In Britain on the day following the German surrender, the country allowed itself a holiday (VE Day) to celebrate the news. In Ramsbury, as in every community across the Kingdom, all manner of celebrations were hastily organised. Flags and bunting were hung across the High Street and for the first time in five years the flag pole was put back in place on the church tower. Once again the Union Flag flew proudly above the village. Loud speakers were erected in the Square and popular tunes of the day were played. At 5.30 p.m. the Methodist band marched to the tree and played anthems, and that evening a victory dance was held in the Memorial Hall. The hall had been decorated by Mrs Olive Winchcombe, helped by her son Dick and niece Mary Day. Dick also helped provide music for the event assisted by John Martin and George Page.

A victory bonfire, courtesy of Norman Day, was started at 10 p.m. on the glebe land north of Whittonditch Road. A torch light procession starting at the tree marched up Oxford Street and Whittonditch Road to the bonfire – the location of which had been kept a closely guarded secret. Flaming torches carried by many in the procession were thrown into the old straw rick upon which sat an effigy of Adolf Hitler.

At long last the people of Ramsbury, with the rest of Britain, could look forward to a lasting peace. Those who had fought so hard for victory in lands near and far could now return home and start to build a 'brave new world'.

Although the appearance of Ramsbury has changed little during the intervening years its character has altered considerably. The villagers no longer rely solely on agriculture for their employment, as the vast majority now find work in towns such as Swindon and Newbury, where they commute on a daily basis.

Today the casual visitor will see little remaining evidence of the events that took place around Ramsbury 50 or more years ago, but hopefully this book will ensure that the village's small, but important role in World War Two will not be forgotten.

The airfield

The site of Ramsbury airfield from the air taken during the summer of 1995. (D. Summers)

During 1994 as a part of the Axford memorial dedication, Ken Wakefield landed his 1944 Piper L-4
Cub aircraft on the old airfield in order to refuel. This gave the photographers present a rare
opportunity to photograph a genuine wartime aircraft at Ramsbury. (C.A. Day)

The memorials

DONATED BY THE YANKS
OF 437TH TROOP CARRIER GROUP
STATIONED ON THE HILL 1944 – 1945

In the square, below the tree, passers by may rest on the two seats donated by veterans of the 437th TCG.
(Author)

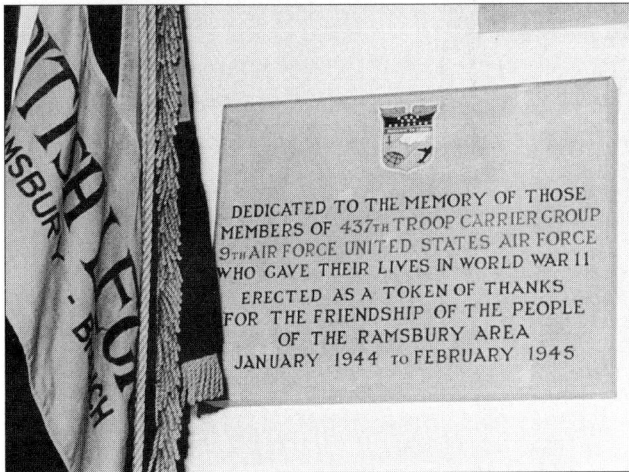

DEDICATED TO THE MEMORY OF THOSE MEMBERS OF 437TH TROOP CARRIER GROUP 9TH AIR FORCE UNITED STATES AIR FORCE WHO GAVE THEIR LIVES IN WORLD WAR II ERECTED AS A TOKEN OF THANKS FOR THE FRIENDSHIP OF THE PEOPLE OF THE RAMSBURY AREA JANUARY 1944 TO FEBRUARY 1945

(Above) In the church this same unit have erected a stone plaque as a token of their friendship towards the people of Ramsbury. (Author)

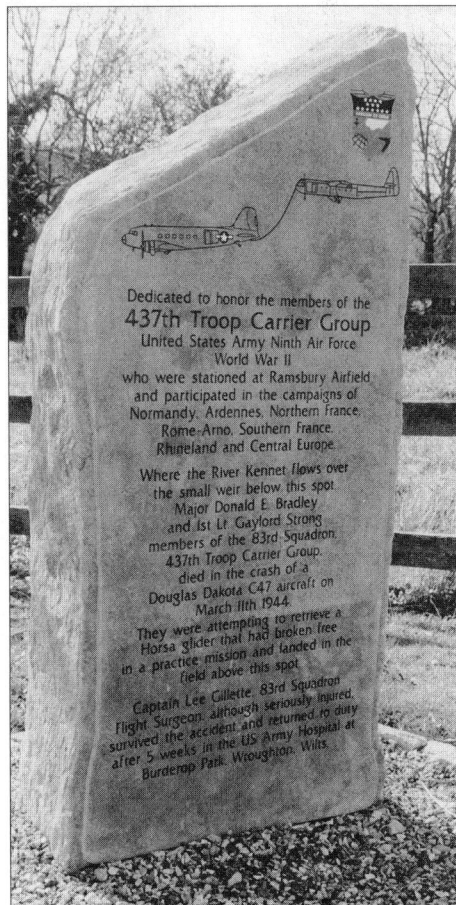

Dedicated to honor the members of the
437th Troop Carrier Group
United States Army Ninth Air Force
World War II
who were stationed at Ramsbury Airfield
and participated in the campaigns of
Normandy, Ardennes, Northern France,
Rome-Arno, Southern France,
Rhineland and Central Europe

Where the River Kennet flows over
the small weir below this spot
Major Donald E. Bradley
and 1st Lt Gaylord Strong
members of the 83rd Squadron,
437th Troop Carrier Group,
died in the crash of a
Douglas Dakota C47 aircraft on
March 11th 1944
They were attempting to retrieve a
Horsa glider that had broken free
in a practice mission and landed in the
field above this spot

Captain Lee Gillette, 83rd Squadron
Flight Surgeon, although seriously injured,
survived the accident and returned to duty
after 5 weeks in the US Army Hospital at
Burderop Park, Wroughton, Wilts

(Right) Two miles away in the village of Axford another memorial recalls the ill-fated crash of 11th March 1944, when a C-47 transport aircraft belonging to the 437th TCG came down in a field near the village killing two of its crew. (Author)

(Above) On 18th June 1999 a bronze plaque, presented to the village by veterans of the 506th Regiment of the 101st Airborne Division, was officially dedicated at the Memorial Hall. US Veteran Joe Beyrle (centre) travelled to England from his home in Michigan especially for the occasion. (C.A. Day)

(Left) In a corner of Ramsbury's churchyard stands this poignant reminder of the sacrifice and tragedy of war. We will remember them. (C.A. Day)

APPENDIX ONE

The 82nd and 101st Airborne Divisions flight movement table from 53rd wing area.

Operation 'Overlord' June 6th 1944

Airborne unit	Troop Carrier Group	No. Aircraft	No. Gliders	Take-off airfield
June 6th 1944 (D-Day)				
502nd Reg less 1st Batt	438th	81	–	Greenham Common
1st Batt 502nd Reg	436th	Not	–	Membury
377th para FA Batt	437th	Known		
326th Medical Coy	(85th Sqd only)			
3rd Batt 501st Reg	435th	45	–	Welford
101st Divisional HQ				
101st Div Sig Coy				
101st Divisional Arty				
101st Divisional HQ	434th	52	52 (CG-4A)	Aldermaston
101st Div Sig Coy				
326th Engineers				
326th Medical Coy				
Bty A&B 81st AA Batt				
101st Divisional HQ	434th	32	32 (Horsa)	Aldermaston
101st Div Sig Coy				
Jeeps for para Reg				
Bty A&B 80th AA Batt	437th	52	52 (CG-4A)	Ramsbury
82nd Divisional HQ	(Less 85th Sqd)			
82nd Divisional Arty				
82nd Div Sig Coy				
Bty C 80th AA Batt	437th	26	8 (CG-4A)	Ramsbury
82nd Divisional HQ	(Less 85th Sqd)		18 (Horsa)	
82nd Div Sig Coy				
82nd Divisional Arty				
HQ 80th AA Batt				
307th Medical Coy	438th	50	14 (CG-4A)	Greenham Common
82nd Recon Plat			36 (Horsa)	
82nd Div Sig Coy				
82nd Divisional HQ				
319th Glider FA Batt	436th	50	2 (CG-4A)	Membury
320th Glider FA Batt			48 (Horsa)	
82nd Divisional Arty				
307th Medical Coy				
Coy A 307th Eng Batt				
320th FA Batt	435th	50	12 (CG-4A)	Welford
			38 (Horsa)	

Airborne Unit	Troop Carrier Group	No. Aircraft	No. Gliders	Take-off Airfield
June 7th 1944 (D-Day plus one)				
1st Batt 325th Gld Reg	437th	50	32 (CG-4A)	Ramsbury
Coy A 307th Eng Batt			18 (Horsa)	
HQ 325th Glider Reg	434th	50	50 (CG-4A)	Aldermaston
HQ Coy 325th Gld Reg				
82nd Divisional Arty				
Coy A 307th Eng Batt				
82nd Recon Plt				

APPENDIX TWO

101st Airborne Division flight movement table
for Operation 'Market Garden'
Holland September 1944

Airborne Unit	Troop Carrier Group	No. Aircraft	No. Gliders	Take-off airfield
September 17th 1944 (D-Day)				
501st Reg less 3rd Batt	434th	90	–	Aldermaston
3rd Batt 501st Reg	442nd	45	–	Chilbolton
3rd Batt 506th Reg		45	–	
506th Reg less 3rd Batt	436th	90	–	Membury
1st Batt 502nd Reg	435th	45	–	Welford
101st Divisonal HQ		9	–	
Coy C 326th Eng		7	–	
Personnel of Div Arty		3	–	
502nd Reg less 1st Batt	438th	90	–	Greenham Common
101st Divisional HQ	437th	8	8	Ramsbury
101st Signal Coy		14	14	
101st Recon Plat		15	15	
326th Medical Coy		6	6	
101st Divisional Arty		3	3	
Jeeps for the three para Regiments		24	24	
September 18th 1944 (D-Day plus one)				
327th Glider Reg	437th	23	23	Ramsbury
101st Divisional HQ		19	19	
101st Div Sig Coy		18	18	
Jeeps for 502nd Reg		8	8	
Jeeps for 501st Reg		2	2	
327th Glider Reg	434th	58	58	Aldermaston
Jeeps for 501st Reg		20	20	
Gen McAuliffe and party		2	2	
326th Medical Coy	435th	54	54	Welford
Jeeps for 502nd Reg		6	6	
Jeeps for 506th Reg	438th	7	7	Greenham Common
Jeeps for 502nd Reg		8	8	
377th Para FA Batt		40	40	
426th Quartermaster Coy		25	25	
326th Engineers	442nd	65	65	Chilbolton
Jeeps for 506th Reg		15	15	
2nd Batt 327th Reg	436th	80	80	Membury

Airborne Unit	Troop Carrier Group	No. Aircraft	No. Gliders	Take-off airfield
September 19th 1944 (D-Day plus two)				
327th Glider Reg	435th	18	18	Welford
101st Divisional Arty		21	21	
377th FA Batt		22	22	
81st AA Batt		1	1	
1st Batt 327th Reg	436th	41	41	Membury
907th FA Batt		40	40	
326th Engineers		1	1	
81st AA Batt	434th	40	40	Aldermaston
321st FA Batt		40	40	
1st Batt 327th Reg	442nd	41	41	Chilbolton
907th FABatt		40	40	
81st AA Batt	438th	40	40	Greenham Common
321st FA Batt		31	31	
907th FA Batt		9	9	
September 20th 1944 (D-Day plus three)				
Bty B 377th Batt	442nd	12	12	Ramsbury

The 437th TCG were originally scheduled to fly this mission. However, due to extenuating circumstances, the 442nd TCG took over. Despite this the mission was still flown from Ramsbury.

Airborne Unit	Troop Carrier Group	No. Aircraft	No. Gliders	Take-off airfield
September 23rd 1944 (D-Day plus six)				
907th FA Batt	438th	20	20	Greenham Common
81st AA Batt		11	11	
101st Signal Coy		3	3	
326th Engineers		1	1	
327th Glider Inf		1	1	
321st FA Batt		1	1	
101st Div Ordnance Coy		1	1	
907th FA Batt	436th	39	39	Membury
327th Glider Inf		8	8	
September 25th 1944 (D-Day plus eight)				
327th Glider Inf	434th			Aldermaston
907th FA Batt				

Bibliography

Listed below are books that I have consulted during my research. To their authors I offer my sincere thanks:

A Bridge Too Far, by Cornelius Ryan (Hamish Hamilton Ltd, 1974)

A Journey to the Far Shore, by Frank Guild jr. (Privately published, 1949)

A Short History of Grove Airfield 1941-1996, by Don Summers (Ridgeway Military & Aviation Research Group, 1997)

A Short History of the 48th Division (Territorial Army), (Privately published 1962)

Action of the Tiger, by Frank Guild jr. (The Battery Press Inc, 1980)

Action Stations, volume 9, by Chris Ashworth (Patrick Stephens Ltd, 1985)

As Eagles Screamed, by Donald R. Burgett (Bantam Books, 1979)

British Airborne Troops, by Barry Gregory (Macdonald & Jane's, 1974)

British Fire Engine Heritage, by Roger Pennington (Reed Books Ltd, 1994)

Channel Islands Occupation Review, edited by Peter Bryans (Channel Islands Occupation Soc, 1985)

Fire Engines, by Trevor Whitehead (Shire Publications Ltd, 1981)

Firemen's Uniforms, by Brian Wright (Shire Publications Ltd, 1991)

Into The Valley, by Col. Charles H. Young (PrintComm, Dallas, USA, 1995)

Prisoners of England, by Miriam Kochan (Macmillan Publishers Ltd, 1985)

Prisoners of War, by Fiona Reynoldson (Wayland Publishing Ltd, 1990)

Rendezvous with Destiny, by Rapport & Northwood (Infantry Journal Press, 1948)

The 9th Air Force in World War II, by Ken C. Rust (Aero Publishers USA, 1970)

The Airspeed Oxford, by D.R. Rawlings (Profile Publications, 1971)

The Anson File, by Ray Sturtivant (Air-Britain Ltd, 1988)

The GI's, by Norman Longmate (Hutchinson & Co. Ltd, 1975)

The Glider War, by James E. Mrazek (Robert Hale & Co Ltd, 1975)

The History of the Wiltshire Home Guard, by E. A. Mackay (Lockbridge, 1946)

The Mighty Eighth, by Roger A. Freeman (Macdonald and Jane's, 1970)

The Paras 1940-1984, by Gregor Ferguson (Reed International Books Ltd, 1984)

The Real Dad's Army, by Norman Longmate (Hutchinson Library Services, 1974)

The Village in the Valley, by Barbara Croucher (Privately published 1986)

UK Airfields of the Ninth Then and Now, by Roger A. Freeman (After the Battle, 1996)

War in the Countryside 1939-1945, by Sadie Ward (Cameron Books in association with David & Charles, 1988)

War Prizes, by Phil Butler (Midland Counties Publications, 1994)